I0504165

The Shopify Millionaire:

A Step-by-Step Guide to Building a Profitable E-Commerce Empire

Table of contents

Chapter 1: Why Shopify is the Perfect Platform for Building an E-Commerce Empire

In today's digital age, starting an e-commerce business has become an increasingly popular way to pursue financial freedom and build a successful empire. Among the numerous e-commerce platforms available, Shopify stands out as one of the most powerful and user-friendly options. In this chapter, we will delve into the reasons why Shopify is the perfect platform for aspiring entrepreneurs looking to create a lucrative e-commerce business.

1.1 Simplicity and User-Friendliness:

One of the key advantages of Shopify is its simplicity and user-friendliness. Whether you have prior technical knowledge or not, Shopify's intuitive interface makes it easy for anyone to set up and manage an online store. Its drag-and-drop functionality allows you to customize your store's design, add products, and manage inventory with minimal effort. Shopify takes care of the technical aspects, such as hosting, security, and software updates, allowing you to focus on growing your business.

1.2 Robust Features and Scalability:

Shopify offers a wide range of built-in features that empower entrepreneurs to build and scale their e-commerce businesses effectively. From inventory management to order fulfillment, payment processing, and shipping integration, Shopify provides a comprehensive toolkit to streamline operations. Moreover, Shopify's App Store offers an extensive selection of plugins and apps that enhance functionality, allowing you to add features and tailor your store to meet specific business needs as you grow.

1.3 Mobile-Optimized and Responsive Design:

With the increasing prevalence of mobile shopping, having a mobile-optimized store is essential. Shopify understands this and offers responsive themes that adapt seamlessly to different screen sizes. This ensures a consistent and enjoyable shopping experience for customers, regardless of the device they are using. Mobile responsiveness is not only important for user experience but also plays a significant role in search engine rankings, as search engines prioritize mobile-friendly websites.

1.4 SEO-Friendly Infrastructure:

Search engine optimization (SEO) is crucial for driving organic traffic to your e-commerce store. Shopify provides a solid foundation for implementing effective SEO strategies. It generates clean and search engine-friendly URLs, allows you to customize meta tags, optimize product descriptions, and create relevant content. Additionally, Shopify's fast page load times and secure hosting contribute to a positive user experience, which can further boost your SEO efforts.

1.5 Seamless Integration with Third-Party Platforms:

Shopify seamlessly integrates with various third-party platforms and services, offering flexibility and extended functionality. You can integrate popular marketing tools, email service providers, analytics platforms, social media platforms, and more to streamline your marketing efforts and gain valuable insights. This integration ecosystem enables you to leverage the power of existing tools and services while utilizing Shopify as the central hub for your e-commerce operations.

1.6 Robust Security and Reliability:

Security is a top priority for any online business. Shopify provides a highly secure infrastructure, protecting your store and customer data from potential threats. As a hosted solution, Shopify takes care of security updates, server maintenance, and backups, ensuring that your store remains operational and secure at all times. This peace of mind allows you to focus on growing your business instead of worrying about technical vulnerabilities.

1.7 Support and Community:

Building an e-commerce business can be challenging, especially for beginners. Shopify offers excellent customer support through multiple channels, including live chat, email, and phone, to assist you with any technical or operational issues. Additionally, Shopify has a vast community of entrepreneurs and experts who share insights, best practices, and success stories. This supportive community provides a valuable resource for knowledge-sharing, networking, and inspiration.

Conclusion:

Shopify's simplicity, robust features, scalability, mobile optimization, SEO-friendliness, integration capabilities, security, and support make it an ideal platform for building an e-commerce empire. Whether you're just starting out or looking to expand an existing business, Shopify provides the tools and resources necessary to create a successful and profitable online store.

Chapter 2: The Mindset of a Successful Shopify Entrepreneur

Building a successful e-commerce business on Shopify requires more than just technical skills and industry knowledge. It demands a specific mindset that sets successful entrepreneurs apart from the rest. In this chapter, we will explore the mindset characteristics that empower individuals to navigate the challenges, persevere through obstacles, and ultimately achieve success in the competitive world of e-commerce.

2.1 Vision and Clarity:

Successful Shopify entrepreneurs possess a clear vision of what they want to achieve with their e-commerce business. They have a deep understanding of their target market, the products they offer, and the value they bring to their customers. By defining a compelling vision, entrepreneurs can align their actions and decisions with their long-term goals, staying focused on the bigger picture and avoiding distractions.

2.2 Resilience and Perseverance:

The journey of building a Shopify business is not without its setbacks and challenges. Successful entrepreneurs understand that failures and obstacles are part of the process and see them as opportunities for growth. They possess resilience, the ability to bounce back from setbacks, learn from failures, and keep moving forward. Perseverance is their driving force, allowing them to stay committed to their goals despite the inevitable ups and downs.

2.3 Adaptability and Innovation:

The e-commerce landscape is constantly evolving, and successful entrepreneurs embrace change. They are adaptable, willing to pivot their strategies and adjust their business models to meet market demands. They proactively seek new opportunities and stay ahead of trends, always looking for innovative ways to differentiate themselves from the competition. This mindset enables them to capitalize on emerging technologies, consumer preferences, and market shifts.

2.4 Continuous Learning and Growth:

A growth mindset is essential for a successful Shopify entrepreneur. They have an insatiable thirst for knowledge and are committed to continuous learning. They stay updated on industry trends, attend conferences and workshops, read relevant books and articles, and engage in networking and mentorship opportunities. This mindset allows them to acquire new skills, stay ahead of the curve, and adapt to the ever-changing e-commerce landscape.

2.5 Risk-Taking and Decision-Making:

Successful entrepreneurs understand that taking calculated risks is a crucial part of business growth. They are comfortable stepping outside their comfort zones and making decisions even in uncertain situations. They weigh the potential rewards against the risks involved and make informed choices. They understand that not all risks will pay off, but they embrace the possibility of failure as an opportunity for learning and growth.

2.6 Customer-Centricity and Relationship Building:

At the core of every successful e-commerce business is a strong focus on the customer. Shopify entrepreneurs prioritize understanding their customers' needs, preferences, and pain points. They strive to deliver exceptional customer experiences, build trust, and foster long-term relationships. They actively seek feedback, listen to customer insights, and iterate their strategies to consistently meet and exceed customer expectations.

2.7 Goal Setting and Action-Oriented Mindset:

Successful Shopify entrepreneurs set clear, measurable goals and break them down into actionable steps. They understand the importance of setting both short-term and long-term objectives to stay motivated and track their progress. Moreover, they have a bias for action, consistently taking steps towards their goals rather than getting stuck in analysis paralysis. They understand that progress is made through consistent action and implementation.

Conclusion:

Developing the mindset of a successful Shopify entrepreneur is crucial for long-term success in the e-commerce world. By cultivating a vision, embracing resilience, adaptability, and continuous learning, taking calculated risks, prioritizing the customer, and setting clear goals, entrepreneurs can navigate challenges and create thriving businesses on Shopify.

Chapter 3: Identifying Your Niche and Target Market

In the vast landscape of e-commerce, identifying a profitable niche and understanding your target market is essential for building a successful Shopify business. In this chapter, we will explore the process of finding your niche, understanding its characteristics, and identifying your target market. By doing so, you will be able to tailor your products, marketing strategies, and customer experiences to meet the specific needs of your target audience.

3.1 Discovering Your Passion and Expertise:

The first step in identifying your niche is to consider your passions, interests, and areas of expertise. What topics or industries ignite your enthusiasm? What knowledge or skills do you possess that can be leveraged in a business? By aligning your e-commerce venture with your passion and expertise, you increase your chances of success and create a foundation for sustainable growth.

3.2 Market Research and Competitive Analysis:

Once you have identified potential niches, it's crucial to conduct thorough market research and competitive analysis. Start by examining the demand and size of the market. Are there existing businesses catering to this niche? What are their strengths and weaknesses? Identify any gaps or underserved segments within the market that you can potentially target.

3.3 Defining Your Unique Selling Proposition (USP):

To stand out in a crowded market, you need a clear and compelling Unique Selling Proposition (USP). Your USP defines what sets your business apart from the competition and why customers should choose your products over others. It could be based on price, product features, quality, customer service, sustainability, or any other differentiating factor. Your USP will play a significant role in attracting and retaining customers within your target market.

3.4 Analyzing Target Market Demographics and Psychographics:

Understanding the demographics and psychographics of your target market is essential for effective marketing and product development. Demographics include factors such as age, gender, location, income level, and occupation, while psychographics delve into deeper aspects such as lifestyle, values, interests, and purchasing behavior. Conduct surveys, interviews, and market research to gather insights and create detailed buyer personas that represent your ideal customers.

3.5 Identifying Pain Points and Needs:

To successfully serve your target market, you must identify their pain points, challenges, and unmet needs. What problems do they face in relation to the niche you're targeting? How can your products or services provide solutions and add value to their lives? By understanding their pain points and needs, you can develop products that resonate with your audience and tailor your marketing messages to address their specific concerns.

3.6 Evaluating Market Trends and Future Growth Potential:

While it's important to focus on the present, considering future market trends and growth potential is equally crucial. Analyze industry reports, stay updated on emerging technologies, and monitor consumer behavior shifts. By identifying and aligning your business with growing trends, you position yourself for long-term success and the ability to adapt as the market evolves.

3.7 Validating Your Niche and Target Market:

Once you have gathered all the necessary information, it's important to validate your niche and target market before investing significant resources. Conduct market tests, pilot launches, or create minimum viable products to gauge interest and collect feedback. This validation process helps ensure that there is a viable market for your products and confirms that your target audience resonates with your value proposition.

Conclusion:

Identifying your niche and target market is a crucial foundation for building a successful Shopify business. By aligning your passions, conducting thorough market research, defining a compelling USP, understanding the demographics and psychographics of your target audience, identifying their pain points and needs, and considering market trends and growth potential, you can position your business for success.

Chapter 4: Conducting Market Research to Validate Your Business Idea

Before diving headfirst into building your Shopify business, it's crucial to conduct thorough market research to validate your business idea. Market research provides valuable insights into your target audience, competition, industry trends, and customer preferences. In this chapter, we will explore the process of conducting market research to ensure that your business idea has a solid foundation and a high potential for success.

4.1 Defining Your Research Objectives:

Start by clearly defining your research objectives. What specific information are you seeking? Are you validating the demand for your product? Assessing the viability of your target market? Evaluating customer preferences or pricing strategies? By clarifying your objectives, you can structure your research effectively and gather the most relevant data.

4.2 Secondary Research:

Begin your market research by conducting secondary research. This involves gathering existing information from reputable sources such as industry reports, market studies, trade publications, government data, and competitor analysis. Secondary research provides a foundation of knowledge about your industry, target market, and competitors, allowing you to understand the broader landscape before diving into primary research.

4.3 Competitor Analysis:

An essential part of market research is conducting a thorough analysis of your competitors. Identify direct and indirect competitors who offer similar products or target the same audience. Analyze their business strategies, pricing models, marketing tactics, strengths, weaknesses, and unique selling propositions. This analysis helps you identify gaps in the market and differentiate your business from existing competitors.

4.4 Primary Research:

Primary research involves gathering firsthand data directly from your target audience. There are several methods you can employ to collect primary research, including surveys, interviews, focus groups, and observation. Design your research instruments to gather specific information that aligns with your research objectives. Primary research allows you to gain valuable insights into customer preferences, pain points, buying behavior, and product feedback.

4.5 Surveys:

Surveys are an effective way to gather quantitative data from a large number of respondents. Design your survey questions to gather information about demographics, preferences, purchasing behavior, and feedback on your business idea or product concept. Utilize online survey tools to distribute your surveys and analyze the data. Consider incentivizing survey participation to encourage a higher response rate.

4.6 Interviews and Focus Groups:

Interviews and focus groups provide a more qualitative approach to gathering insights. Conduct one-on-one interviews or group discussions with individuals from your target audience. Ask open-ended questions to delve deeper into their thoughts, opinions, and experiences. These interactions provide valuable qualitative data and can uncover insights that surveys may not capture.

4.7 Observation and User Testing:

Observation involves directly observing how your target audience interacts with existing products, both online and offline. User testing allows you to test your product with a sample group and gather real-time feedback on its usability, functionality, and overall experience. By observing and testing, you can identify potential improvements and ensure that your product meets the needs of your target audience.

4.8 Analyzing and Interpreting Data:

Once you have collected the data from your primary research, it's crucial to analyze and interpret it effectively. Utilize data analysis tools or software to uncover patterns, trends, and insights. Look for common themes, identify customer preferences, and draw conclusions based on the data collected. These findings will help you make informed decisions about your business idea and refine your strategies.

4.9 Validating and Iterating Your Business Idea:

Based on the insights gathered from your market research, assess the viability and potential of your business idea. Consider the demand, competition, customer preferences, and market trends. If the research validates your idea, it's time to move forward and refine your business plan accordingly. However, if the research indicates challenges or gaps in your idea, be open to iterating and making necessary adjustments to increase your chances of success.

Conclusion:

Conducting thorough market research is an essential step in validating your business idea and ensuring its potential for success. By conducting secondary research, analyzing competitors, gathering primary research through surveys, interviews, and observation, and effectively analyzing and interpreting the data, you can make informed decisions about your business concept. Use the insights gained from market research to refine your business plan, differentiate yourself from competitors, and tailor your products and marketing strategies to meet the needs of your target audience.

Chapter 5: Finding Products to Sell on Shopify

One of the key factors for a successful Shopify business is offering products that resonate with your target audience. In this chapter, we will explore various strategies and methods for finding products to sell on your Shopify store. By sourcing the right products, you can attract customers, drive sales, and build a profitable e-commerce business.

5.1 Define Your Product Criteria:

Before diving into product sourcing, it's important to define your product criteria. Consider factors such as quality, uniqueness, market demand, profit margin, and compatibility with your brand. By establishing clear criteria, you can narrow down your options and focus on finding products that align with your business goals and target audience.

5.2 Research Trending Products:

Stay updated on current market trends and consumer preferences to identify potentially popular products. Utilize social media platforms, online forums, industry publications, and trend-tracking tools to gain insights into emerging trends and popular products. Analyze their market demand and evaluate their potential fit with your target audience.

5.3 Conduct Competitor Analysis:

Analyze your competitors to identify products that are performing well in your niche. Visit competitor websites, browse their product catalogs, and monitor their best-selling items. This analysis can help you gain insights into the products that resonate with your target audience and uncover potential gaps in the market that you can fill.

5.4 Utilize Supplier Directories and Marketplaces:

Supplier directories and marketplaces offer a wide range of products from various suppliers and manufacturers. Platforms like Alibaba, Oberlo, and AliExpress provide access to a vast selection of products that you can source for your Shopify store. Explore different categories, read product reviews, and compare prices and shipping options to find suitable products for your business.

5.5 Consider Dropshipping:

Dropshipping is a popular fulfillment method where you partner with suppliers who handle inventory and shipping. This allows you to focus on marketing and customer acquisition without the need for upfront inventory investment. Research dropshipping suppliers, evaluate their product offerings, reliability, and customer service. Platforms like Oberlo, Modalyst, and Spocket offer extensive product catalogs and integrations with Shopify.

5.6 Source Locally or Create Unique Products:

Consider sourcing products locally or creating unique products to differentiate your business. Local sourcing supports your community and allows you to offer unique or handmade items that may appeal to your target audience. Attend trade shows, visit local artisans, and establish relationships with local suppliers. Alternatively, explore product customization or private labeling options to create exclusive products under your brand.

5.7 Analyze Customer Feedback and Reviews:

Pay attention to customer feedback and product reviews on various e-commerce platforms and social media channels. Identify products that receive positive feedback and high ratings from customers. This feedback can guide you in selecting products that meet the expectations and preferences of your target audience.

5.8 Test and Validate:

Before committing to large product orders, consider testing and validating the market demand for your selected products. Start with a smaller inventory or utilize pre-order campaigns to gauge customer interest. This approach helps mitigate risks and ensures that you invest in products with proven market demand.

5.9 Build Relationships with Suppliers:

Establishing strong relationships with your suppliers is crucial for smooth operations and reliable product sourcing. Communicate your expectations, negotiate pricing and terms, and ensure they align with your business goals. Building a mutually beneficial relationship with your suppliers can lead to better product availability, support, and potential partnership opportunities.

Conclusion:

Finding the right products to sell on your Shopify store is a critical step in building a successful e-commerce business. By defining your product criteria, researching trending products, analyzing competitors, utilizing supplier directories and marketplaces, considering dropshipping, sourcing locally or creating unique products, analyzing customer feedback, and testing the market, you can identify products that resonate with your target audience and have a high potential for success.

Chapter 6: Sourcing Products: Wholesale vs. Dropshipping vs. Private Labeling

Once you have identified the products you want to sell on your Shopify store, it's crucial to determine the most suitable sourcing method. In this chapter, we will explore three popular options: wholesale, dropshipping, and private labeling. Each method has its own advantages and considerations, and understanding them will help you make informed decisions about product sourcing for your Shopify business.

6.1 Wholesale Sourcing:

Wholesale sourcing involves purchasing products in bulk directly from manufacturers or distributors at a discounted price. This method requires upfront investment and storage space for inventory. Here are some key considerations for wholesale sourcing:

a) Establishing Relationships with Suppliers:

Identify reputable suppliers who offer the products you want to sell. Attend trade shows, industry events, or utilize online directories to connect with potential suppliers. Building strong relationships with your suppliers is crucial for reliable product availability, pricing negotiation, and potential partnership opportunities.

b) Evaluating Pricing and Minimum Order Quantities (MOQs):

When sourcing wholesale products, carefully consider the pricing structure and minimum order quantities (MOQs) set by the suppliers. Evaluate the profitability of selling the products at the wholesale price and determine if the MOQs align with your business needs and storage capabilities.

c) Managing Inventory and Fulfillment:

With wholesale sourcing, you have control over inventory management and fulfillment. You will be responsible for storing, organizing, and shipping the products to customers. Consider warehousing options, inventory tracking systems, and fulfillment strategies to ensure efficient operations.

d) Quality Control and Product Inspections:

As you purchase products in bulk, it's essential to prioritize quality control. Conduct product inspections, request samples, and establish clear quality standards with your suppliers. This helps maintain customer satisfaction and minimize returns or product issues.

6.2 Dropshipping:

Dropshipping is a fulfillment method where you partner with suppliers who handle inventory and shipping. Here are key considerations for dropshipping:

a) Supplier Selection and Integration:

Research and select reliable dropshipping suppliers that offer the products you want to sell. Ensure they have a seamless integration with your Shopify store or utilize dropshipping platforms like Oberlo, Modalyst, or Spocket.

Assess their product range, fulfillment capabilities, and customer service.

b) No Upfront Inventory Investment:

One of the advantages of dropshipping is that you don't need to invest in upfront inventory. When a customer places an order on your Shopify store, the supplier ships the product directly to the customer. This model reduces financial risk and allows you to focus on marketing and customer acquisition.

c) Profit Margins and Competitive Pricing:

Since dropshipping products are sourced from suppliers, profit margins can be lower compared to wholesale sourcing or private labeling. Evaluate pricing structures and shipping costs to ensure competitive pricing while maintaining profitability. Consider offering value-added services or bundling products to differentiate your offerings.

d) Communication and Customer Service:

Maintain open lines of communication with your suppliers to address any product or order-related inquiries from customers. Establish clear expectations regarding shipping times, tracking information, and returns. Providing excellent customer service and timely communication can help build trust and loyalty with your customers.

6.3 Private Labeling:

Private labeling involves creating your own brand and applying it to products sourced from manufacturers. Here are key considerations for private labeling:

a) Product Customization and Branding:

Select products that can be customized or branded with your own logo, packaging, and labels. Work closely with manufacturers to ensure your branding requirements are met. This allows you to differentiate your products and create a unique brand identity.

b) Manufacturer Selection and Quality Assurance:

Research and identify reliable manufacturers who can produce the desired products with high quality. Conduct due diligence, request product samples, and ensure they have a track record of delivering consistent quality. Establish clear specifications and quality control processes to maintain product standards.

c) MOQs and Inventory Management:

Manufacturers often have MOQs for private labeling. Evaluate the MOQs based on your business needs and storage capabilities. Manage inventory effectively to avoid overstocking or running out of products. Consider forecasting demand, utilizing inventory management software, and establishing reorder points.

d) Building Brand Reputation and Marketing:

Private labeling allows you to build a unique brand and focus on creating a strong brand reputation. Develop a marketing strategy that highlights the value, quality, and uniqueness of your private label products. Leverage content marketing, social media, and influencer partnerships to promote your brand and attract customers.

Conclusion:

When sourcing products for your Shopify store, carefully evaluate the pros and cons of wholesale sourcing, dropshipping, and private labeling. Consider factors such as upfront investment, inventory management, fulfillment, branding opportunities, profit margins, and scalability. Each method offers different advantages and considerations, so choose the sourcing method that aligns with your business goals, resources, and target audience.

Chapter 7: Evaluating and Choosing Your Suppliers

Choosing the right suppliers for your Shopify business is crucial for maintaining product quality, ensuring timely deliveries, and establishing a strong foundation for success. In this chapter, we will discuss the process of evaluating and selecting suppliers to source your products. By following these guidelines, you can build reliable partnerships that contribute to the growth and profitability of your business.

7.1 Supplier Evaluation Criteria:

Before evaluating potential suppliers, it's important to establish criteria that align with your business goals and product requirements. Consider the following factors when evaluating and choosing your suppliers:

a) Product Quality and Reliability:

Product quality is paramount for customer satisfaction and brand reputation. Assess the quality standards of suppliers by requesting samples or inspecting existing products. Ensure that the supplier can consistently meet your quality expectations and adhere to any industry-specific certifications or standards.

b) Production Capacity and Lead Times:

Evaluate suppliers' production capacity to ensure they can meet your demand and deliver products within the required timelines. Consider lead times, production capabilities, and their ability to handle volume fluctuations. Timely deliveries are crucial to maintain inventory levels and meet customer expectations.

c) Pricing and Cost Structure:

Analyze the pricing structure of potential suppliers to ensure it aligns with your budget and profit margins. Compare pricing quotes, including manufacturing costs, shipping fees, and any additional charges. Seek suppliers that offer competitive pricing without compromising quality.

d) Communication and Responsiveness:

Effective communication is vital for a successful supplier relationship. Assess the supplier's responsiveness, willingness to address inquiries or concerns, and ability to provide timely updates. A reliable supplier should be accessible and maintain clear lines of communication.

e) Ethical and Sustainable Practices:

Consider suppliers that uphold ethical and sustainable practices. Evaluate their commitment to fair labor practices, environmental sustainability, and social responsibility. Aligning with suppliers who share similar values can contribute to your brand's image and resonate with conscious consumers.

7.2 Supplier Research and Due Diligence:

Once you have established your evaluation criteria, conduct thorough research to identify potential suppliers. Here are key steps to follow during the research and due diligence process:

a) Online Searches and Directories:

Utilize search engines, online directories, and industry-specific platforms to discover potential suppliers. Visit their websites, review their product offerings, and gather initial information about their capabilities and expertise.

b) Supplier References and Reviews:

Seek references from industry peers, attend trade shows, or join professional networks to gather recommendations and insights about suppliers. Additionally, search for online reviews or testimonials from other businesses that have worked with the suppliers. This feedback can provide valuable information about their reliability and customer satisfaction.

c) Supplier Background Checks:

Conduct background checks on potential suppliers to ensure their legitimacy and financial stability. Verify their business licenses, certifications, and check if they have any history of legal issues or disputes. This step helps minimize risks and establish trustworthiness.

d) Request Samples and Conduct Product Testing:

Request samples from potential suppliers to assess the quality of their products firsthand. Conduct product testing to verify their adherence to specifications and quality standards. This step ensures that the products meet your requirements before committing to a supplier.

7.3 Supplier Evaluation and Selection:

Based on your research and due diligence, it's time to evaluate and select the most suitable suppliers for your business. Consider the following steps during the evaluation and selection process:

a) Supplier Scoring and Comparison:

Develop a scoring system or matrix to objectively evaluate and compare potential suppliers. Assign weights to the evaluation criteria and rate each supplier accordingly. This approach allows you to make informed decisions based on quantifiable data.

b) Request Detailed Proposals:

Request detailed proposals from the top-rated suppliers to gain further insights into their capabilities, pricing, lead times, and terms. Review and compare these proposals to ensure they align with your business requirements and objectives.

c) Conduct Supplier Interviews:

Interview the shortlisted suppliers to assess their communication skills, responsiveness, and compatibility with your business values. Ask relevant questions about their production processes, quality control measures, and ability to handle volume fluctuations.

e) Negotiate Terms and Contracts:

Once you have identified the preferred supplier(s), negotiate the terms and conditions of your partnership. Discuss pricing, lead times, payment terms, and any other specific requirements. Draft a clear contract that outlines the agreed-upon terms and protects the interests of both parties.

f) Monitor and Reassess Suppliers:

Continuously monitor the performance of your suppliers to ensure they meet your expectations. Regularly assess their adherence to quality standards, on-time deliveries, and communication. Be prepared to reassess and explore alternative suppliers if any issues arise.

Conclusion:

Choosing reliable suppliers is a critical step in establishing a successful Shopify business. By evaluating suppliers based on criteria such as product quality, production capacity, pricing, communication, and ethical practices, you can forge strong partnerships that contribute to the growth and success of your business. Take the time to conduct thorough research, due diligence, and evaluations to make informed decisions when selecting your suppliers.

Chapter 8: Setting Up Your Shopify Store

Your Shopify store serves as the foundation for your e-commerce business. In this chapter, we will guide you through the process of setting up your Shopify store effectively. From choosing the right theme to optimizing your product listings, we'll cover essential steps to create a visually appealing and user-friendly online store that maximizes conversions and drives sales.

8.1 Choosing the Right Theme:

The theme you choose for your Shopify store sets the overall look and feel of your website. Consider the following factors when selecting a theme:

a) Visual Appeal and Brand Alignment:

Choose a theme that reflects your brand's identity and resonates with your target audience. Pay attention to the color scheme, typography, and overall design elements. A visually appealing theme helps create a positive first impression and builds trust with your visitors.

b) Responsiveness and Mobile-Friendliness:

Ensure the theme you select is mobile-responsive, as an increasing number of customers shop using mobile devices. A responsive design adapts to different screen sizes, providing a seamless browsing experience and improving overall customer satisfaction.

c) Customization and Flexibility:

Consider the level of customization options available with each theme. Look for themes that allow you to customize layouts, fonts, colors, and sections to tailor your store's appearance to your brand. Flexibility in theme customization enables you to create a unique and personalized online store.

d) Support and Updates:

Choose a theme from reputable developers who provide regular updates and offer customer support. Regular updates ensure compatibility with Shopify's latest features and address any security or performance issues. Prompt and reliable support can assist you in troubleshooting any theme-related challenges.

8.2 Configuring Store Settings:

Once you've chosen your theme, it's time to configure your store settings. Pay attention to the following areas:

a) General Store Information:

Enter your store name, address, and contact information in the general settings. This information will be displayed on your website and helps customers reach out to you if needed.

b) Payment Gateways:

Set up your payment gateways to enable smooth transactions. Shopify offers various payment options, including Shopify Payments, which streamlines the payment process. Additionally, integrate popular third-party payment gateways like PayPal, Stripe, or Authorize.net based on your customers' preferences.

c) Shipping Methods and Rates:

Define your shipping methods and rates in accordance with your products and target audience. Consider factors such as shipping carriers, delivery speeds, and international shipping options. Offer transparent shipping costs and provide estimated delivery times to manage customer expectations.

d) Tax Settings:

Configure your tax settings based on your business's location and applicable tax regulations. Shopify provides automated tax calculations, simplifying the process for you. Consult with a tax professional to ensure compliance with local tax laws.

8.3 Adding and Organizing Product Listings:

Your product listings are the core of your Shopify store. Optimize your product listings to attract customers and drive sales:

a) Compelling Product Descriptions:

Write informative and persuasive product descriptions that highlight the key features, benefits, and unique selling points. Use clear and concise language, include relevant keywords, and address potential customer concerns or questions.

b) High-Quality Product Images:

Include high-quality product images that showcase your products from various angles. Use professional photography or high-resolution images to enhance visual appeal and provide an accurate representation of your products.

c) Detailed Product Variants:

If your products come in different sizes, colors, or variations, clearly outline the available options and allow customers to select their preferred variants. Provide accurate information about pricing, stock availability, and any additional charges for specific variants.

d) Customer Reviews and Ratings:

Enable customer reviews and ratings to build trust and social proof. Positive reviews can significantly influence purchase decisions. Encourage customers to leave reviews by offering incentives or sending follow-up emails post-purchase.

8.4 Optimizing User Experience and Navigation:

A seamless user experience encourages visitors to explore your store and make purchases. Implement the following strategies to optimize user experience:

a) Clear Navigation Menus:

Design intuitive navigation menus that categorize your products logically. Ensure customers can easily find what they're looking for and navigate between different sections of your store.

b) Search Functionality:

Incorporate a search bar to enable customers to find specific products quickly. Implement search filters to refine search results based on product attributes like price, color, or size.

c) Simple and Streamlined Checkout Process:

Minimize the number of steps required for customers to complete their purchase. Implement a simplified and user-friendly checkout process, including guest checkout options, autofill features, and progress indicators.

d) Fast Loading Speed:

Optimize your store's loading speed by compressing images, minimizing unnecessary scripts or plugins, and utilizing a reliable hosting provider. A fast-loading website improves user experience and reduces bounce rates.

Conclusion:

Setting up your Shopify store effectively is a crucial step towards building a successful e-commerce business. Choose a visually appealing theme that aligns with your brand, configure store settings accurately, and optimize your product listings for maximum impact. Focus on providing a seamless user experience and optimizing navigation to drive conversions.

Chapter 9: Customizing Your Shopify Store to Maximize Sales

Once your Shopify store is set up, customizing it to maximize sales becomes essential. In this chapter, we will explore effective strategies and techniques to customize your store and create a compelling shopping experience for your customers. From branding and design to optimizing product pages, these customization methods will help drive conversions and boost your sales.

9.1 Branding Your Store:

Branding plays a crucial role in establishing a strong identity and building customer trust. Customize your store's branding elements:

a) Logo and Color Scheme:

Design a professional logo that represents your brand's identity. Choose a color scheme that aligns with your brand personality and creates visual consistency throughout your store.

b) Typography and Fonts:

Select fonts that are legible and reflect your brand's style. Consistent typography enhances the overall aesthetics and readability of your store.

c) Brand Messaging and Voice:

Craft a compelling brand story and establish a consistent brand voice. Use this voice in your product descriptions, blog posts, and communication with customers to create a cohesive brand experience.

9.2 Optimizing Product Pages:

Product pages are crucial for converting visitors into customers. Customize your product pages to optimize their impact:

a) High-Quality Product Images:

Include multiple high-quality images that showcase your products from different angles. Use zoom features to allow customers to examine product details closely.

b) Clear and Persuasive Product Descriptions:

Write compelling product descriptions that highlight the key features, benefits, and unique selling points. Use persuasive language and address customer pain points or concerns.

c) Customer Reviews and Ratings:

Display customer reviews and ratings prominently on product pages. Positive reviews build trust and encourage potential customers to make a purchase.

d) Upselling and Cross-Selling Opportunities:

Utilize upselling and cross-selling techniques to increase the average order value. Recommend related products or offer bundle deals on product pages to entice customers to add more items to their cart.

9.3 Enhancing User Experience:

A seamless and enjoyable user experience keeps customers engaged and encourages repeat purchases. Customize your store to enhance user experience:

a) Responsive Design:

Ensure your store is mobile-responsive to provide a consistent and user-friendly experience across different devices. Test your store's responsiveness on various screen sizes to guarantee optimal display.

b) Intuitive Navigation:

Simplify navigation by using clear menus, categorizing products effectively, and implementing a search function. Customers should be able to find products easily and navigate through your store without confusion.

c) Streamlined Checkout Process:

Optimize your checkout process to minimize friction and increase conversions. Remove unnecessary steps, provide guest checkout options, and offer multiple payment gateways for convenience.

d) Personalization and Product Recommendations:

Implement personalized product recommendations based on customer browsing history and purchase behavior. Utilize automation tools and algorithms to suggest relevant products that align with their preferences.

9.4 Adding Trust Signals:

Building trust is crucial for converting visitors into customers. Customize your store to incorporate trust signals:

a) Secure Payment Icons:

Display recognized payment icons and SSL certificates to assure customers that their transactions are secure. Trust in the payment process encourages customers to complete their purchases.

b) Trust Badges and Seals:

Include trust badges and seals from reputable security and privacy organizations to instill confidence in your store. Trust seals indicate that your store meets certain industry standards and safeguards customer data.

c) Return Policy and Guarantees:

Clearly communicate your return policy and any guarantees offered to customers. A transparent and customer-friendly return policy builds trust and encourages confident purchases.

Conclusion:

Customizing your Shopify store is crucial for maximizing sales and creating a memorable shopping experience for your customers. Pay attention to branding, optimize product pages, enhance user experience, and incorporate trust signals to build customer trust and encourage conversions. Regularly evaluate and update your customization strategies based on customer feedback and data analysis.

Chapter 10: Creating Product Pages that Convert

The product page is the final destination for potential customers on your Shopify store. It's where the magic happens—where visitors become buyers. In this chapter, we will explore the key elements and strategies for creating product pages that effectively convert visitors into customers. From persuasive product descriptions to captivating visuals, we'll cover everything you need to know to optimize your product pages for maximum conversions.

10.1 Compelling Product Descriptions:

The product description is your opportunity to showcase the value and benefits of your products. Craft persuasive and informative descriptions that captivate your audience:

a) Highlight Key Features:

Identify the unique selling points of your products and highlight them in your descriptions. Clearly communicate how your products solve customer problems or meet their needs.

b) Use Descriptive Language:

Utilize vivid and engaging language to paint a picture of how customers' lives can be improved by using your products. Create an emotional connection by appealing to their desires and aspirations.

c) Address Customer Pain Points:

Identify common pain points or objections that customers may have and address them directly in your product descriptions. Show how your products provide solutions or alleviate those concerns.

d) Incorporate Social Proof:

Include testimonials or customer reviews within your product descriptions to build trust and credibility. Authentic customer experiences can influence potential buyers and increase confidence in their purchasing decision.

10.2 Captivating Visuals:

Visual elements play a crucial role in capturing customers' attention and enticing them to make a purchase. Optimize your product visuals for maximum impact:

a) High-Quality Product Images:

Invest in professional product photography or use high-resolution images that accurately represent your products. Show multiple angles, zoom capabilities, and any unique product features.

b) Lifestyle Images:

Include lifestyle images that showcase your products in real-world settings. This helps customers visualize themselves using your products and creates a sense of aspiration.

c) Product Videos:

Consider creating product videos that demonstrate the features, functionality, or benefits of your products. Videos can engage customers and provide a more immersive experience.

d) Infographics or Visual Guides:

If applicable, use infographics or visual guides to explain complex features or usage instructions. Visual aids can make information more digestible and enhance the overall user experience.

10.3 Clear Call-to-Action (CTA):

A strong and visible call-to-action is crucial for guiding customers towards the next step in the purchasing process. Optimize your CTAs to drive conversions:

a) Use Action-Oriented Language:

Ensure your CTA buttons use compelling and action-oriented language that encourages immediate action. Examples include "Add to Cart," "Buy Now," or "Get Yours Today."

b) Place CTAs Strategically:

Position your CTAs prominently on the page, typically near the top and bottom, as well as within the product description. Make them easily visible and accessible to customers at all times.

c) Create Urgency and Scarcity:

Incorporate urgency-inducing elements, such as limited-time offers or low stock notifications, to create a sense of urgency and drive customers to take immediate action.

10.4 Detailed Product Information:

Provide comprehensive and accurate information about your products to alleviate customer concerns and facilitate informed purchasing decisions:

a) Specifications and Dimensions:

Include detailed specifications, dimensions, materials, and any other relevant product information. This helps customers assess whether the product meets their requirements.

b) Pricing and Discounts:

Clearly display the price of your products, any applicable discounts, and any additional costs such as shipping fees or taxes. Transparency in pricing builds trust and eliminates surprises at checkout.

c) Size Guides and Sizing Charts:

If applicable, include size guides or sizing charts to assist customers in selecting the correct size. This reduces the likelihood of returns and enhances customer satisfaction.

d) Frequently Asked Questions (FAQs):

Anticipate common customer questions and provide answers in an easily accessible FAQ section. Addressing potential concerns or doubts can help customers make confident purchasing decisions.

Conclusion:

Creating product pages that convert is crucial for driving sales on your Shopify store. Craft persuasive and informative product descriptions, use captivating visuals, optimize your call-to-action, and provide comprehensive product information. Continuously monitor and test different elements of your product pages to optimize their performance.

Chapter 11: Optimizing Your Checkout Process to Boost Conversions

The checkout process is the final hurdle between a customer's intent to purchase and the completion of the transaction. In this chapter, we will delve into the key strategies and techniques for optimizing your checkout process to boost conversions on your Shopify store. From simplifying the steps to building trust and reducing friction, we will cover essential elements to create a seamless and conversion-focused checkout experience.

11.1 Simplify the Checkout Steps:

A complex and lengthy checkout process can deter customers from completing their purchases. Streamline your checkout process to remove unnecessary barriers and enhance user experience:

a) Guest Checkout Option:

Offer a guest checkout option that allows customers to make a purchase without creating an account. Many customers prefer a quick and hassle-free checkout process, especially for their first purchase.

b) Minimize Form Fields:

Request only essential information during checkout. Reduce the number of form fields to fill out, focusing on capturing information necessary for order fulfillment and communication.

c) Progress Indicators:

Display progress indicators during the checkout process, indicating the steps required to complete the purchase. This helps customers understand where they are in the process and reduces uncertainty.

d) One-Page Checkout:

Consider implementing a one-page checkout system where customers can review and complete their purchase on a single page. This eliminates the need for customers to navigate through multiple steps, reducing friction.

11.2 Offer Multiple Payment Options:

Providing a variety of payment options caters to customers' preferences and increases the likelihood of completing a purchase. Integrate popular and secure payment gateways to enhance customer convenience:

a) Shopify Payments:

Enable Shopify Payments as a primary payment option. Shopify Payments offers a seamless integration and simplifies the payment process for both you and your customers.

b) Popular Third-Party Payment Gateways:

Integrate widely recognized payment gateways like PayPal, Stripe, or Amazon Pay to provide additional payment options. These trusted gateways enhance customer trust and offer familiar payment methods.

c) Digital Wallets:

Consider integrating digital wallets such as Apple Pay or Google Pay to cater to customers who prefer quick and secure payment options. Digital wallets streamline the checkout process, reducing friction.

11.3 Build Trust and Security:

Building trust and ensuring a secure checkout environment are crucial for encouraging customers to proceed with their purchase. Implement trust-building elements to instill confidence:

a) Secure Checkout Badges:

Display security badges, SSL certificates, or trust seals prominently during the checkout process. These visual indicators reassure customers that their personal and financial information is protected.

b) Clear Privacy Policy:

Link to a transparent and easily accessible privacy policy that outlines how customer data is collected, stored, and used. Clearly communicate your commitment to data protection and customer privacy.

c) Customer Reviews and Testimonials:

Include customer reviews and testimonials on your checkout page. Positive feedback from satisfied customers reinforces trust and social proof, boosting confidence in the purchasing decision.

d) Secure and Reliable Hosting:

Ensure your website is hosted on a secure and reliable server. A reliable hosting provider with robust security measures minimizes the risk of technical issues or data breaches during the checkout process.

11.4 Streamline Mobile Checkout:

Mobile devices play a significant role in e-commerce, and optimizing your checkout process for mobile users is crucial. Create a mobile-friendly checkout experience to cater to the growing mobile customer base:

a) Responsive Design:

Ensure your checkout page is fully responsive, adapting to different screen sizes and orientations. Test your checkout process thoroughly on various mobile devices to ensure a seamless experience.

b) Simplified Input Methods:

Optimize the input methods for mobile users, such as using mobile-friendly form fields, autocomplete features, and numeric keypads for numerical input. Simplify the data entry process to reduce friction.

c)   Mobile Payment Options:

Integrate mobile payment options like Apple Pay or Google Pay to allow customers to complete their purchase with a single tap. Mobile payment methods enhance convenience and encourage mobile conversions.

Conclusion:

Optimizing your checkout process is crucial for maximizing conversions on your Shopify store. Simplify the steps, offer multiple payment options, build trust, and streamline the mobile checkout experience. Regularly monitor your checkout analytics, gather customer feedback, and make data-driven improvements to continually enhance your checkout process.

Chapter 12: Setting Up Payment Processing and Shipping

Setting up payment processing and shipping methods are vital steps in establishing a smooth and efficient e-commerce operation. In this chapter, we will explore the key considerations and strategies for configuring payment processing and shipping on your Shopify store. From choosing payment gateways to defining shipping zones and rates, we will cover essential elements to ensure a seamless transaction and delivery process for your customers.

12.1 Choosing Payment Gateways:

Payment gateways facilitate the secure transfer of funds between your customers and your business. Consider the following factors when selecting payment gateways for your Shopify store:

a) Shopify Payments:

Shopify Payments is a convenient and integrated payment solution provided by Shopify. It offers competitive rates and simplifies the setup process. Consider enabling Shopify Payments as it seamlessly integrates with your store.

b) Third-Party Payment Gateways:

Integrate popular third-party payment gateways, such as PayPal, Stripe, or Authorize.Net, to provide additional payment options. Research their fees, compatibility with your target market, and the countries they support.

c)   Consider Customer Preferences:

Take into account your target audience's payment preferences. Offer payment options that cater to their needs, such as credit cards, debit cards, digital wallets, or local payment methods popular in their region.

d)   Security and Fraud Prevention:

Ensure the payment gateways you choose prioritize security measures and offer fraud prevention features. Protecting customer data and preventing fraudulent transactions are paramount for building trust.

12.2 Configuring Shipping Settings:

Shipping is a critical aspect of your e-commerce business. Configuring accurate and efficient shipping settings helps provide a positive customer experience. Consider the following when setting up shipping options:

a) Define Shipping Zones:

Divide your target regions into shipping zones based on their geographic location. Determine specific shipping rates and methods for each zone. This approach allows for accurate shipping cost calculation.

b) Shipping Methods:

Choose appropriate shipping methods that align with your products and customer expectations. Common options include standard shipping, expedited shipping, free shipping thresholds, or local pickup.

c) Carrier Integration:

Integrate shipping carriers such as USPS, FedEx, UPS, or DHL to automate shipping label generation and package tracking. Carrier integration streamlines your shipping workflow and enhances customer satisfaction.

d) Shipping Rates and Calculations:

Configure shipping rates based on factors like weight, dimensions, destination, and shipping method. Set up real-time carrier rates or flat-rate shipping options depending on your business model and customer preferences.

12.3 Handling International Shipping:

Expanding your reach to international customers requires special considerations. Ensure a smooth international shipping process by addressing the following:

a) Customs and Duties:

Familiarize yourself with international customs regulations and duties. Provide clear information to customers about potential additional charges they may incur upon delivery.

b) International Shipping Options:

Explore shipping services that specialize in international deliveries, such as ePacket, FedEx International, or DHL Express. Research their rates, delivery times, and tracking capabilities to find the best fit for your business.

c) Localized Checkout Experience:

Optimize your checkout process for international customers by offering multi-currency options, translating key elements of the checkout page, and displaying accurate shipping costs in their local currency.

d) Address Verification:

Implement address verification tools to minimize shipping errors and ensure accurate delivery. Use address validation services to validate addresses provided by international customers.

Conclusion:

Setting up payment processing and shipping methods correctly is crucial for a successful e-commerce operation. Choose payment gateways that meet customer preferences and prioritize security. Configure accurate shipping settings, define shipping zones, and integrate with reliable carriers. Consider international shipping if expanding your customer base globally. Regularly review and optimize your payment and shipping setup to provide a seamless and trustworthy experience for your customers.

Chapter 13: Building Trust and Credibility with Your Customers

Building trust and credibility with your customers is paramount for the success of your Shopify store. In this chapter, we will explore strategies and techniques to establish trust, foster strong customer relationships, and enhance your store's credibility. From providing exceptional customer service to leveraging social proof, we will cover essential elements to build a reputable and trustworthy brand.

13.1 Exceptional Customer Service:

Providing exceptional customer service is a fundamental pillar of building trust. Focus on the following aspects to deliver an outstanding customer experience:

a) Prompt and Responsive Communication:

Respond to customer inquiries, concerns, and support requests in a timely manner. Offer multiple communication channels, such as email, live chat, or phone, to accommodate different preferences.

b) Personalized Interactions:

Treat each customer as an individual. Address them by name, personalize your communications, and demonstrate a genuine interest in their needs. Personalization helps create a positive and memorable experience.

c) Clear Policies and Terms:

Ensure your store's policies and terms are clearly communicated and easily accessible. This includes return policies, shipping information, warranties, and any relevant terms and conditions. Transparent policies build trust and manage customer expectations.

d) Hassle-Free Returns and Refunds:

Make the return and refund process as seamless as possible. Provide clear instructions and support for customers who wish to return or exchange products. Simplify the refund process to minimize customer frustration.

13.2 Social Proof:

Leveraging social proof is an effective way to build trust and credibility. Showcase positive experiences and feedback from satisfied customers:

a) Customer Reviews and Testimonials:

Display customer reviews and testimonials prominently on your website. Encourage satisfied customers to leave reviews and share their experiences. Genuine and positive reviews build trust and influence potential buyers.

b) Influencer Partnerships:

Collaborate with influencers or industry experts who align with your brand. Their endorsement and positive reviews can significantly impact customer trust and drive sales.

c) Social Media Mentions:

Monitor social media platforms for mentions of your brand. Engage with customers, respond to their feedback, and address any concerns publicly. Demonstrating your commitment to customer satisfaction on social media builds trust.

13.3 Security and Privacy:

Ensuring the security of customer data and respecting their privacy is crucial in building trust in the digital landscape:

a) Secure Website and Transactions:

Implement SSL encryption on your website to secure customer data during transactions. Clearly communicate your security measures, such as secure checkout badges and SSL certificates, to instill confidence in your customers.

b) Privacy Policy and Data Protection:

Create a comprehensive privacy policy that outlines how customer data is collected, stored, and used. Clearly state your commitment to data protection and compliance with relevant regulations.

c) PCI Compliance:

Adhere to Payment Card Industry Data Security Standard (PCI DSS) requirements if you handle credit card information. Demonstrating your compliance assures customers that their payment data is handled securely.

13.4 Authentic Branding and Storytelling:

Establish an authentic brand identity and tell your story in a compelling way. This helps customers connect with your brand and builds trust over time:

a) Brand Values and Mission:

Clearly articulate your brand's values and mission. Share your story and the purpose behind your business. This humanizes your brand and fosters a deeper connection with your audience.

b) Transparent Company Information:

Share information about your company, such as its history, team members, and location. Providing transparent company details helps customers feel more comfortable and confident in engaging with your brand.

c) Social Responsibility and Sustainability:

Highlight any social responsibility initiatives or sustainability practices your business embraces. Demonstrating your commitment to positive social and environmental impact enhances your brand's credibility.

Conclusion:

Building trust and credibility with your customers is a continuous process that requires attention to detail and a customer-centric approach. Provide exceptional customer service, leverage social proof, prioritize security and privacy, and establish an authentic brand identity. Consistently deliver on your promises and adapt to meet customer expectations. By building trust, you foster long-lasting customer relationships and establish your Shopify store as a reputable and reliable brand.

Chapter 14: Developing a Brand Identity and Voice

Developing a strong brand identity and voice is crucial for establishing a distinct and memorable presence in the marketplace. In this chapter, we will explore strategies and techniques for crafting a compelling brand identity and voice for your Shopify store. From defining your brand's values to creating consistent messaging, we will cover essential elements to differentiate your brand and resonate with your target audience.

14.1 Defining Your Brand Identity:

Your brand identity represents the unique qualities and characteristics that define your business. Consider the following steps to develop a strong brand identity:

a) Identify Your Brand Values:

Define the core values that guide your business. These values should align with your mission and reflect what your brand stands for. Clearly articulate these values and use them as a compass for decision-making.

b) Understand Your Target Audience:

Gain a deep understanding of your target audience's preferences, needs, and aspirations. Tailor your brand identity to resonate with their desires and values. This alignment creates a stronger connection with your audience.

c) Craft Your Brand Story:

Develop a compelling brand story that communicates your journey, vision, and purpose. Your story should engage and emotionally resonate with your audience, forging a meaningful connection with your brand.

d) Define Your Brand Personality:

Consider the personality traits that best represent your brand. Is your brand playful, sophisticated, or trustworthy? Define the tone and characteristics that will be consistent throughout your communication channels.

14.2 Creating a Consistent Brand Voice:

Your brand voice is the tone and style in which you communicate with your audience. Consistency in your brand voice helps establish familiarity and builds trust. Follow these guidelines to develop a consistent brand voice:

a) Understand Your Audience's Language:

Familiarize yourself with the language and communication styles that resonate with your target audience. Use the appropriate tone, vocabulary, and expressions that align with their preferences and expectations.

b) Define Your Tone:

Choose a consistent tone for your brand voice. Whether it's friendly, professional, casual, or authoritative, ensure that it remains consistent across all your communication channels and interactions.

c) Develop Brand Guidelines:

Create brand guidelines that outline the specific dos and don'ts of your brand voice. This includes guidelines for writing style, grammar usage, punctuation, and any unique language or jargon associated with your brand.

d) Train Your Team:

Educate your team members, especially those responsible for customer interactions, on your brand voice. Ensure that they understand and embody the desired tone and style when communicating with customers.

14.3 Visual Branding:

Visual elements play a crucial role in conveying your brand identity. Consistent visual branding helps customers recognize and remember your brand. Consider the following aspects:

a) Logo and Typography:

Design a visually appealing and memorable logo that represents your brand identity. Choose typography that complements your brand voice and conveys the desired message.

b) Color Palette:

Select a cohesive color palette that reflects your brand's personality and resonates with your target audience. Consistency in color usage creates visual harmony and strengthens brand recognition.

c) Imagery and Graphics:

Choose imagery and graphics that align with your brand identity. Whether it's through photography, illustrations, or graphic elements, ensure that they evoke the desired emotions and convey your brand's essence.

d) Consistent Branding Across Channels:

Maintain consistent visual branding across all touchpoints, including your website, social media profiles, packaging, and marketing materials. Consistency fosters brand recognition and builds trust.

Conclusion:

Developing a strong brand identity and voice is essential for creating a memorable and differentiated presence in the marketplace. Define your brand values, craft your brand story, and create a consistent brand voice that resonates with your target audience. Establish visual branding elements that reflect your brand's personality and maintain consistency across all channels. By developing a cohesive brand identity and voice, you will strengthen customer recognition, build brand loyalty, and position your Shopify store for long-term success.

Chapter 15: Creating a Content Marketing Strategy to Drive Traffic to Your Store

A well-executed content marketing strategy can significantly boost traffic to your Shopify store and attract potential customers. In this chapter, we will explore the key components and best practices for creating an effective content marketing strategy. From defining your target audience to selecting content formats and channels, we will cover essential elements to drive organic traffic and engage your audience.

15.1 Defining Your Target Audience:

Understanding your target audience is the foundation of a successful content marketing strategy. Consider the following steps to define your target audience:

a) Demographics:

Identify the key demographics of your target audience, including age, gender, location, and occupation. This information will help tailor your content to their specific needs and preferences.

b) Psychographics:

Dig deeper into your target audience's psychographics, such as their interests, values, behaviors, and motivations. This insight allows you to create content that resonates with their desires and aspirations.

c) Pain Points and Challenges:

Identify the pain points and challenges your target audience faces related to your industry or niche.

Understanding their problems enables you to create valuable and relevant content that addresses their needs.

d) Content Consumption Habits:

Determine how your target audience consumes content. Are they active on social media? Do they prefer reading blogs or watching videos? This knowledge helps you select the most effective content formats and channels.

15.2 Selecting Content Formats:

Choosing the right content formats is crucial for engaging your audience and driving traffic. Consider the following popular content formats for your strategy:

a) Blog Posts:

Create informative and engaging blog posts that address your audience's pain points, provide solutions, and showcase your expertise. Optimize your blog posts for search engines to drive organic traffic.

b) Videos:

Produce videos that educate, entertain, or demonstrate your products. Video content is highly engaging and shareable, making it an effective way to attract and retain your target audience.

c) Infographics:

Design visually appealing infographics that present complex information in a concise and engaging manner.

Infographics are highly shareable and can drive traffic when used in blog posts or social media.

d) E-books and Guides:

Create comprehensive e-books or guides that provide in-depth information on topics relevant to your target audience. Offer them as downloadable resources in exchange for email sign-ups to build your email list.

e) Podcasts:

Host a podcast where you discuss industry trends, interview experts, or share valuable insights. Podcasts are a popular medium that allows you to reach and engage with your audience on-the-go.

15.3 Choosing Content Distribution Channels:

Selecting the right content distribution channels is essential for reaching your target audience effectively. Consider the following channels for distributing your content:

a) Website and Blog:

Publish your content on your Shopify store's blog or website. Optimize it for search engines to improve visibility and attract organic traffic.

b) Social Media Platforms:

Leverage social media platforms like Facebook, Instagram, Twitter, LinkedIn, or Pinterest to share and promote your content. Tailor your content to each platform's unique features and audience preferences.

c) Email Marketing:

Utilize your email list to distribute your content directly to your subscribers. Send regular newsletters or email updates featuring your latest blog posts, videos, or e-books.

d) Guest Posting:

Write guest posts for other relevant blogs or websites in your industry. This allows you to tap into their audience and drive traffic back to your store through an author bio or link.

e) Influencer Collaboration:

Collaborate with influencers or industry experts to co-create or promote your content. Their endorsement and reach can significantly expand your content's visibility and attract new audiences.

f) Content Promotion and SEO:

Creating great content is not enough; you also need to promote it effectively and optimize it for search engines. Consider the following strategies:

f.1/ Social Media Promotion:

Share your content regularly on social media platforms. Encourage your audience to engage, comment, and share your content, amplifying its reach.

f.2/ SEO Optimization:

Optimize your content for search engines by incorporating relevant keywords, meta tags, and descriptive URLs. This improves your content's visibility in search engine results and drives organic traffic.

f.3 /Backlinking:

Build backlinks to your content by reaching out to relevant websites or bloggers in your industry. Guest posting, influencer collaborations, or participating in industry forums can help you acquire valuable backlinks.

f.4 /Repurposing Content:

Repurpose your existing content into different formats to reach a wider audience. For example, turn a blog post into a video or create an infographic based on your e-book. This maximizes the value of your content and expands its reach.

Conclusion:

A well-crafted content marketing strategy can drive organic traffic, engage your audience, and establish your brand as an authority in your industry. Define your target audience, select appropriate content formats, and choose the right distribution channels to reach your audience effectively. Promote your content through social media, SEO optimization, and strategic partnerships. By consistently delivering valuable and relevant content, you will attract more visitors to your Shopify store and increase your chances of converting them into loyal customers.

Chapter 16: Creating a Social Media Strategy to Promote Your Brand

Social media has become a powerful tool for brand promotion and customer engagement. In this chapter, we will explore the key components and best practices for creating an effective social media strategy to promote your brand and drive traffic to your Shopify store. From choosing the right platforms to developing engaging content, we will cover essential elements to help you harness the potential of social media.

16.1 Choosing the Right Social Media Platforms:

Not all social media platforms are created equal, and it's essential to select the ones that align with your target audience and brand objectives. Consider the following steps:

a) Research Your Target Audience:

Identify the social media platforms your target audience is most active on. Analyze their demographics, interests, and behavior to determine where your brand can effectively reach and engage them.

b) Assess Platform Relevance:

Evaluate each platform's suitability for your brand. Consider factors such as the platform's user base, content formats supported, and the alignment between your brand's voice and the platform's culture.

c) Focus on Key Platforms:

Instead of spreading yourself thin across multiple platforms, focus on a few key platforms that offer the best potential for reaching and engaging your target audience effectively.

d) Monitor Industry Trends:

Stay updated on emerging platforms and shifts in user behavior. Regularly assess the relevance and effectiveness of your chosen platforms to ensure you're maximizing your social media efforts.

16.2 Developing Engaging Content:

Creating compelling and shareable content is crucial for building brand awareness and fostering audience engagement. Consider the following strategies:

a) Understand Your Audience's Interests:

Research and understand what kind of content resonates with your target audience. Identify their pain points, desires, and interests, and tailor your content to provide value and meet their needs.

b) Mix Content Formats:

Diversify your content formats to cater to different preferences. Experiment with images, videos, infographics, user-generated content, and interactive elements to keep your audience engaged and excited.

c) Craft Engaging Captions:

Write captivating captions that grab attention, evoke emotions, and encourage interaction. Use storytelling techniques, humor, or thought-provoking questions to spark conversations and encourage sharing.

d) User-Generated Content:

Encourage your audience to create and share content related to your brand. User-generated content not only increases engagement but also serves as social proof and authenticates your brand.

16.3 Creating a Content Calendar:

Developing a content calendar helps you stay organized and ensures a consistent flow of content. Consider the following steps:

a) Plan Ahead:

Outline a content calendar for each social media platform, taking into account key dates, holidays, and industry events. Plan your content in advance to maintain a steady stream of posts.

b) Maintain Consistency:

Establish a consistent posting schedule that aligns with your audience's expectations and the platform's best practices. Consistency helps maintain visibility and engagement.

c) Mix Content Types:

Create a diverse mix of content, including promotional posts, educational content, behind-the-scenes glimpses, user-generated content features, and interactive polls or contests.

d) Track Performance:

Regularly evaluate your content's performance using analytics tools provided by the social media platforms. Identify which content resonates the most with your audience and adjust your strategy accordingly.

16.4 Engaging with Your Audience:

Engagement is key to building strong relationships with your audience. Actively respond to comments, messages, and mentions to foster a sense of community. Consider the following tips:

a) Respond Promptly:

Reply to comments and messages in a timely manner. Show genuine interest, answer questions, and address concerns. This demonstrates your brand's commitment to customer satisfaction.

b) Encourage User Participation:

Initiate conversations and encourage user participation by asking questions, running polls, or requesting feedback. This not only boosts engagement but also provides valuable insights for your brand.

c) Personalize Interactions:

Use the personalization features provided by social media platforms to address users by name and tailor your responses to their specific queries or comments. Personalized interactions help create a memorable and positive brand experience.

d) Monitor Brand Mentions:

Keep track of brand mentions and hashtags related to your business. Respond to positive mentions to express gratitude, and address negative mentions promptly and professionally to manage your brand's reputation.

Conclusion:

A well-crafted social media strategy can amplify your brand's reach, increase brand awareness, and drive traffic to your Shopify store. Choose the right platforms, develop engaging content, and create a content calendar to maintain a consistent presence. Actively engage with your audience and foster meaningful interactions. Regularly analyze performance metrics to refine your strategy and optimize your social media efforts.

Chapter 17: Building an Email List and Email Marketing Campaigns

Building an email list and implementing effective email marketing campaigns are powerful strategies to engage your audience, nurture customer relationships, and drive sales. In this chapter, we will explore the key components and best practices for building an email list and creating impactful email marketing campaigns to maximize the potential of your Shopify store.

17.1 Building an Email List:

Building a quality email list is essential for reaching a targeted audience who has already shown interest in your brand. Consider the following strategies to grow your email list:

a) Opt-In Forms:

Place opt-in forms strategically on your website and Shopify store. Offer incentives such as exclusive discounts, free resources, or newsletters to encourage visitors to subscribe to your email list.

b) Pop-Up Forms:

Use pop-up forms with exit-intent triggers or timed delays to capture visitors' attention and prompt them to sign up for your email list before leaving your site.

c) Lead Magnets:

Create valuable lead magnets, such as e-books, guides, or exclusive content, that require users to provide their email addresses to access. This helps incentivize email sign-ups.

d) Social Media Promotion:

Promote your email list on social media platforms by directing your followers to sign up for exclusive offers and updates through a dedicated landing page.

e) Contests and Giveaways:

Run contests or giveaways that require participants to provide their email addresses for entry. This can help attract new subscribers and generate buzz around your brand.

17.2 Designing Effective Email Marketing Campaigns:

Crafting compelling and targeted email marketing campaigns can help you nurture customer relationships, drive traffic, and increase sales. Consider the following best practices:

a) Define Campaign Objectives:

Clearly define the objectives for each email marketing campaign. Whether it's promoting a new product, sharing valuable content, or offering special discounts, having a clear objective helps guide your campaign strategy.

b) Segmentation and Personalization:

Segment your email list based on factors such as demographics, purchase history, or engagement level.

Personalize your emails to address each segment's specific needs, interests, and preferences.

c) Engaging Subject Lines:

Craft compelling subject lines that grab the recipient's attention and entice them to open the email. Use personalization, urgency, curiosity, or value propositions to make your subject lines stand out.

d) Valuable and Relevant Content:

Deliver valuable content that resonates with your audience. Whether it's educational articles, product recommendations, or exclusive offers, provide content that adds value and helps build trust.

e) Call-to-Action (CTA):

Include clear and compelling CTAs in your emails that guide recipients towards the desired action, such as making a purchase, downloading a resource, or visiting your Shopify store.

f) Mobile-Friendly Design:

Ensure your email templates are responsive and optimized for mobile devices. A significant portion of email opens occur on mobile, and a seamless mobile experience is essential for maximizing engagement.

g) A/B Testing:

Experiment with different elements of your email campaigns, such as subject lines, visuals, CTAs, or send times. Conduct A/B tests to identify the most effective variations and continuously optimize your campaigns.

17.3 Automation and Email Sequences:

Implement email automation to streamline your communication and deliver personalized experiences. Consider the following automation and email sequence ideas:

a) Welcome Emails:

Send a series of welcome emails to new subscribers, introducing your brand, providing valuable resources, and guiding them towards making their first purchase.

b) Abandoned Cart Reminders:

Set up automated emails to remind customers about their abandoned carts and entice them to complete their purchase by offering incentives, such as discounts or free shipping.

c) Post-Purchase Follow-ups:

Send automated emails after a purchase to thank customers, request feedback, and provide additional product recommendations or exclusive offers to encourage repeat purchases.

d) Re-Engagement Campaigns:

Identify inactive subscribers and launch re-engagement campaigns to win them back. Offer personalized incentives, exclusive content, or special promotions to reignite their interest.

Conclusion:

Building an email list and implementing effective email marketing campaigns are essential for engaging your audience, nurturing relationships, and driving sales. Employ strategies like opt-in forms, lead magnets, and social media promotion to grow your email list. Craft compelling email campaigns by defining objectives, segmenting your audience, and delivering valuable and relevant content. Leverage email automation and sequences to streamline communication and deliver personalized experiences. Continuously test and optimize your campaigns to maximize their effectiveness.

Chapter 18: Leveraging Influencer Marketing to Grow Your Brand

In today's digital age, influencer marketing has emerged as a powerful strategy for expanding brand reach, building credibility, and driving sales. In this chapter, we will explore the key components and best practices for leveraging influencer marketing to grow your brand and attract new customers to your Shopify store.

18.1 Understanding Influencer Marketing:

Influencer marketing involves collaborating with individuals who have a significant following and influence in your target market. These influencers can help promote your brand, products, or services to their engaged audience. Consider the following steps to effectively leverage influencer marketing:

a)   Define Your Goals:

Clearly define your goals for influencer marketing. Are you looking to increase brand awareness, drive sales, or build credibility? Identifying your goals will help you choose the right influencers and measure the success of your campaigns.

b)   Identify Relevant Influencers:

Research and identify influencers who align with your brand values, target audience, and industry. Consider factors such as their follower demographics, engagement rates, content quality, and brand collaborations.

c) Micro-Influencers vs. Macro-Influencers:

Consider working with micro-influencers who have a smaller but highly engaged following. They often have a more niche audience and can provide a more authentic and targeted reach compared to macro-influencers with larger followings.

d) Authenticity and Alignment:

Ensure that the influencers you choose are genuinely interested in your brand and products. Look for alignment between their content and your brand's values to maintain authenticity and resonate with their audience.

18.2 Crafting Effective Influencer Campaigns:

Creating successful influencer campaigns requires careful planning and collaboration. Consider the following best practices:

a) Set Clear Expectations:

Communicate your campaign goals, deliverables, and expectations to the influencers. Establish clear guidelines on content creation, posting frequency, and any required disclosures to maintain transparency and compliance.

b) Authentic and Creative Content:

Encourage influencers to create authentic, creative, and engaging content that showcases your brand and products in a compelling way. Allow them creative freedom while aligning with your brand's messaging.

c) Sponsored Posts and Product Reviews:

Sponsored posts and product reviews are common formats for influencer campaigns. Provide influencers with necessary product information, samples, or access to your Shopify store to facilitate authentic reviews and recommendations.

d) Giveaways and Contests:

Collaborate with influencers to run giveaways or contests that encourage their audience to engage with your brand. This can help increase brand awareness, followers, and drive traffic to your Shopify store.

18.3 Tracking and Measuring Results:

To gauge the effectiveness of your influencer marketing efforts, it's crucial to track and measure key metrics. Consider the following strategies:

a) Track Performance Metrics:

Monitor key performance metrics such as reach, engagement, website traffic, conversions, and sales attributed to influencer campaigns. Utilize tools like UTM parameters and affiliate tracking to attribute sales accurately.

b) Analyze Engagement and Sentiment:

Evaluate the engagement and sentiment generated by influencer posts. Assess comments, likes, shares, and brand mentions to gauge the impact of the collaboration on audience perception and interest.

c) ROI Calculation:

Calculate the return on investment (ROI) of your influencer campaigns by comparing the campaign costs with the generated sales, website traffic, or other relevant metrics. This will help you assess the campaign's profitability.

18.4 Building Long-Term Relationships:

Nurturing long-term relationships with influencers can be beneficial for your brand's growth. Consider the following strategies:

a) Provide Ongoing Support:

Offer continued support and resources to influencers, such as exclusive discounts, sneak peeks of new products, or access to brand events. This helps maintain their interest and commitment to your brand.

b) Collaboration and Co-Creation:

Involve influencers in collaborative efforts, such as product development, content creation, or event participation. This fosters a sense of ownership and strengthens the partnership.

c) Engage in Influencer Advocacy:

Encourage influencers to become brand advocates by sharing their positive experiences with your products or services. User-generated content and testimonials can further amplify your brand's reach and credibility.

Conclusion:

Influencer marketing can be a game-changer for growing your brand and attracting new customers to your Shopify store. Define your goals, identify relevant influencers, and craft compelling campaigns that align with your brand values. Monitor and measure the results to gauge the effectiveness of your influencer collaborations. Nurture long-term relationships with influencers to foster ongoing brand advocacy and partnership.

Chapter 19: Crafting Compelling Product Descriptions and Marketing Copy

In the competitive world of e-commerce, compelling product descriptions and persuasive marketing copy can make all the difference in capturing the attention of potential customers and driving conversions. In this chapter, we will explore the key strategies and best practices for crafting compelling product descriptions and marketing copy that entice and engage your audience on your Shopify store.

19.1 Understanding Your Target Audience:

Before diving into writing product descriptions and marketing copy, it's crucial to have a deep understanding of your target audience. Consider their demographics, preferences, pain points, and motivations. This knowledge will help you tailor your messaging to resonate with their needs and desires.

19.2 Product Descriptions That Sell:

Crafting effective product descriptions requires a balance of informative details and persuasive language. Consider the following strategies:

a) Highlight Unique Selling Points:

Identify and highlight the unique features, benefits, and value propositions of your products. Communicate how your products solve a problem or enhance the customer's life in a compelling way.

b) Use Descriptive and Engaging Language:

Paint a vivid picture with your words, using descriptive language to help customers visualize using or owning your products. Create an emotional connection by appealing to their senses and aspirations.

c) Focus on Benefits, Not Just Features:

While it's important to mention product features, emphasize the benefits and outcomes that customers will experience by using your products. Highlight how your products fulfill their desires, solve their problems, or improve their lives.

d) Use Social Proof:

Incorporate social proof elements such as customer testimonials, ratings, and reviews to build trust and credibility. Showcase positive experiences and outcomes to instill confidence in potential customers.

e) Make it Scannable:

Structure your product descriptions in a way that is easy to read and scan. Use bullet points, subheadings, and concise paragraphs to break up the text and make key information stand out.

19.3 Persuasive Marketing Copy:

In addition to product descriptions, persuasive marketing copy is essential for driving engagement and conversions. Consider the following strategies:

a) Compelling Headlines and Subheadings:

Craft attention-grabbing headlines and subheadings that pique curiosity, highlight key benefits, or address customer pain points. Use persuasive language and power words to captivate your audience.

b) Create a Sense of Urgency:

Incorporate urgency in your marketing copy by emphasizing limited-time offers, exclusive deals, or product scarcity. Communicate the benefits of acting quickly to create a sense of FOMO (fear of missing out).

c) Storytelling:

Tell captivating stories that evoke emotions and create a connection between your brand and your audience. Share narratives that demonstrate how your products have made a positive impact on customers' lives.

d) Use Persuasive Language and Calls-to-Action (CTAs):

Use persuasive language to communicate the value, benefits, and unique selling points of your products. Clearly communicate the desired action with strong CTAs that prompt customers to make a purchase, sign up, or learn more.

e) Test and Optimize:

Continuously test different variations of your marketing copy to determine what resonates best with your audience. Experiment with different headlines, CTAs, or storytelling techniques, and analyze the performance metrics to optimize your messaging.

Conclusion:

Crafting compelling product descriptions and persuasive marketing copy is essential for engaging your audience, building desire, and driving conversions on your Shopify store. Understand your target audience and tailor your messaging to their needs and desires. Highlight unique selling points, focus on benefits, and use social proof to build trust. Create attention-grabbing headlines, incorporate urgency, and tell compelling stories. Continuously test and optimize your copy to maximize its effectiveness.

Chapter 20: Designing Eye-Catching Graphics and Visuals for Your Store

In the visually-driven world of e-commerce, the design of your Shopify store plays a crucial role in capturing the attention of potential customers and creating a memorable brand experience. In this chapter, we will explore the key strategies and best practices for designing eye-catching graphics and visuals that enhance the aesthetic appeal and usability of your store.

20.1 Establishing a Visual Brand Identity:

Before diving into the design process, it's important to establish a cohesive visual brand identity that aligns with your brand values and resonates with your target audience. Consider the following strategies:

a) Define Your Brand Elements:

Identify and define the key visual elements that represent your brand, such as color palette, typography, logo, and imagery style. Consistency across these elements creates a strong and recognizable brand identity.

b) Reflect Your Brand Personality:

Consider your brand's personality and target audience when choosing design elements. Are you aiming for a modern and sleek look or a playful and vibrant vibe? Ensure that your visual design reflects your brand's personality.

c) Incorporate Brand Storytelling:

Use visuals to tell your brand's story and convey its values. Showcase the essence of your brand through imagery that evokes emotions and connects with your audience on a deeper level.

20.2 Creating Attention-Grabbing Banners and Sliders:

Banners and sliders are prime real estate for capturing attention and showcasing promotions or key products. Consider the following strategies:

a) Use High-Quality Imagery:

Utilize high-resolution, professional-quality images that accurately represent your products or convey the desired message. Blurry or low-quality visuals can undermine your brand's credibility.

b) Engaging Call-to-Action (CTA):

Include clear and compelling CTAs in your banners and sliders that prompt visitors to take action, such as "Shop Now," "Learn More," or "Get Started." Make the CTA buttons stand out with contrasting colors.

c) Keep it Simple and Focused:

Avoid cluttering your banners and sliders with excessive text or visuals. Keep the design clean and focused, highlighting a single key message or product to avoid overwhelming the viewer.

20.3 Designing Clear and Intuitive Navigation:

Navigation is a critical aspect of user experience on your Shopify store. Consider the following strategies to design clear and intuitive navigation:

a) Keep it Consistent:

Maintain consistent navigation elements throughout your store, including the header, menu, and footer. This ensures that visitors can easily navigate and find what they're looking for, regardless of the page they're on.

b) Use Clear Labels:

Use clear and descriptive labels for navigation categories and subcategories. Avoid jargon or ambiguous terms that may confuse visitors. Test your navigation with real users to ensure its clarity and ease of use.

c) Visual Hierarchy:

Utilize visual hierarchy techniques to prioritize important navigation elements. Use size, color, or placement to guide the user's attention to the most important categories or pages.

20.4 Optimizing Product Images:

Product images are central to the success of your Shopify store. Consider the following strategies for optimizing product images:

a) High-Quality and Consistent:

Ensure that your product images are of high-quality, displaying the product from different angles and perspectives. Consistency in image style, background, and lighting creates a cohesive and professional look.

b) Zoom and Multiple Views:

Include features that allow customers to zoom in on product images or view them in a larger format. Offer multiple views or alternate product images to provide a comprehensive understanding of the product.

c) Contextual Usage:

Where applicable, show your products in context or in use. This helps customers visualize how the product fits into their lives and enhances their understanding of its features and benefits.

20.5 Mobile-Friendly Design:

Given the increasing number of users accessing e-commerce stores through mobile devices, it's crucial to design visuals that are mobile-friendly. Consider the following strategies:

20.5.1 Responsive Design:

Ensure that your store's design and visuals adapt seamlessly to different screen sizes and resolutions. Test your store on various mobile devices to ensure a consistent and user-friendly experience.

20.5.2 Clear and Readable Text:

Optimize text size and font choices for mobile readability. Avoid using small or intricate fonts that may be difficult to read on smaller screens.

20.5.3 Mobile-Specific Considerations:

Take advantage of mobile-specific features such as touch gestures, swipeable image galleries, and collapsible menus to enhance the mobile user experience and engagement.

Conclusion:

Designing eye-catching graphics and visuals for your Shopify store is essential for capturing the attention of potential customers and creating a memorable brand experience. Establish a cohesive visual brand identity, create attention-grabbing banners and sliders, and design clear and intuitive navigation. Optimize product images to showcase your products effectively and ensure mobile-friendly design for a seamless user experience.

Chapter 21: Creating High-Quality Product Photography and Video

In the world of e-commerce, high-quality product photography and video are essential for showcasing your products in the best possible light and capturing the attention of potential customers. In this chapter, we will explore the key strategies and best practices for creating compelling and professional product photography and video content for your Shopify store.

21.1 Importance of High-Quality Visual Content:

High-quality visual content plays a crucial role in building trust, conveying product details, and enticing customers to make a purchase. Consider the following strategies to create visually appealing product photography and video:

a) Visual Storytelling:

Use product photography and video to tell a compelling story about your products. Showcase how your products can enhance the lives of your customers and evoke emotions that resonate with your target audience.

b) Conveying Product Details:

Ensure that your visual content accurately represents the features, colors, textures, and dimensions of your products. Provide multiple angles and close-ups to give customers a comprehensive understanding of what they can expect.

c) Building Trust:

High-quality visual content instills trust and credibility in your brand. Invest in professional photography and video production to demonstrate that you value the quality and presentation of your products.

21.2 Professional Product Photography:

Capturing high-quality product images requires careful planning and attention to detail. Consider the following strategies:

a) Equipment and Lighting:

Invest in a good camera, tripod, and lighting equipment to capture sharp, well-lit images. Natural light or studio lighting setups can help highlight product details and colors accurately.

b) Background and Props:

Choose a clean and uncluttered background that complements your product. Consider using props or lifestyle elements to create context and make the product more relatable to your target audience.

c) Composition and Framing:

Compose your product shots thoughtfully, considering the rule of thirds and balancing negative space. Experiment with different angles, perspectives, and focal lengths to create visually interesting compositions.

d) Image Editing and Retouching:

Use professional image editing software to enhance your product images. Adjust brightness, contrast, and color balance to ensure accurate representation. Remove any imperfections or distractions that may detract from the product.

21.3 Compelling Product Videos:

Product videos provide an immersive and dynamic way to showcase your products. Consider the following strategies for creating compelling product videos:

a) Storytelling and Scripting:

Develop a script or outline that communicates the key features, benefits, and value of your product. Incorporate storytelling elements to engage and captivate your audience throughout the video.

b) Demonstrations and Product Usage:

Showcase your product in action by demonstrating its use and highlighting its unique features. This helps customers visualize how the product can benefit them and provides a more engaging experience.

c) Professional Video Production:

Invest in professional videography equipment or hire a videographer to ensure high-quality production. Pay attention to lighting, audio quality, and smooth camera movements to create a polished and professional video.

d) Video Length and Optimization:

Keep your product videos concise and focused, typically ranging from 30 seconds to a few minutes. Optimize your videos for web and mobile viewing by compressing file sizes without compromising quality.

21.4 Consistency Across Visual Assets:

Maintain consistency in the style, tone, and branding of your product photography and videos. This creates a cohesive visual experience and reinforces your brand identity. Consider developing style guidelines or templates to streamline the creation process.

Conclusion:

Creating high-quality product photography and video content is essential for showcasing your products in the best possible light and engaging your audience on your Shopify store. Focus on visual storytelling, conveying product details, and building trust through professional production. Invest in equipment, lighting, and editing tools to capture stunning product images. Develop compelling product videos that demonstrate product usage and highlight unique features. Maintain consistency across your visual assets to reinforce your brand identity.

Chapter 22: Using A/B Testing to Optimize Your Store's Performance

Optimizing your Shopify store is an ongoing process that involves continuously improving its performance and conversion rates. A/B testing is a powerful technique that allows you to compare different variations of your store elements to determine which ones yield better results. In this chapter, we will explore the concept of A/B testing and how you can leverage it to optimize your store's performance.

22.1 Understanding A/B Testing:

A/B testing, also known as split testing, involves creating two or more variations of a webpage or specific elements within it and comparing their performance against each other. It helps you make data-driven decisions by measuring the impact of changes on key metrics, such as conversion rates, click-through rates, or average order value.

22.2 Identifying Elements to Test:

To get started with A/B testing, it's crucial to identify the elements of your store that have the potential to impact performance. Consider the following elements for testing:

a) Call-to-Action Buttons:

Test different variations of button colors, sizes, text, and placement to determine which combination generates the highest click-through and conversion rates.

b) Headlines and Product Descriptions:

Experiment with different headlines, product descriptions, and formatting styles to assess which version drives better engagement and encourages more purchases.

c) Pricing and Promotions:

Test different pricing strategies, discount offers, and promotional messages to understand how they affect customer behavior and purchase decisions.

d) Visual Elements:

Evaluate the impact of different product images, banners, sliders, and overall visual design on customer engagement, trust, and conversion rates.

22.3 Setting Up A/B Tests:

Once you have identified the elements to test, follow these steps to set up your A/B tests:

a) Define Your Hypothesis:

Start by formulating a hypothesis about the expected impact of the changes you plan to make. For example, "Changing the color of the call-to-action button to red will increase click-through rates by 10%."

b) Create Test Variations:

Create two or more variations of the element you want to test, ensuring that they differ by only one variable at a time. For example, if testing button color, create one variation with a red button and another with a blue button.

c) Randomize Traffic:

Randomly assign visitors to each variation to ensure unbiased results. This can be done using A/B testing software or platforms specifically designed for this purpose.

d) Measure and Analyze Results:

Track and analyze the performance of each variation using key metrics, such as conversion rates, bounce rates, or revenue. Ensure you have a sufficient sample size to draw statistically significant conclusions.

e) Implement the Winning Variation:

Once you have collected enough data and identified the winning variation, implement it as the new default version on your store.

22.4 Testing Best Practices:

To ensure accurate and reliable results from your A/B tests, consider the following best practices:

a) Test One Variable at a Time:

To isolate the impact of each change, test only one variable at a time. This allows you to determine precisely which element is responsible for the observed results.

b) Test on a Significant Sample Size:

Ensure that your tests are conducted on a sufficiently large sample size to obtain statistically significant results. Small sample sizes may lead to unreliable or misleading conclusions.

c) Test for an Appropriate Duration:

Allow your tests to run for an appropriate duration to capture variations in user behavior across different days, times, or customer segments. Avoid prematurely ending tests before collecting enough data.

d) Continuously Iterate and Test:

A/B testing is an iterative process. Once you have implemented a winning variation, identify new elements or ideas to test and continue optimizing your store for better performance.

Conclusion:

A/B testing is a valuable tool for optimizing your Shopify store's performance and conversion rates. By systematically testing different variations of store elements, you can make data-driven decisions that drive better results. Identify key elements to test, set up experiments, measure results, and implement winning variations. Follow best practices to ensure reliable and accurate outcomes.

Chapter 23: Analyzing Your Shopify Store's Metrics and Key Performance Indicators (KPIs)

Analyzing your Shopify store's metrics and key performance indicators (KPIs) is crucial for understanding the effectiveness of your marketing efforts, identifying areas for improvement, and making data-driven decisions. In this chapter, we will explore the key metrics and KPIs to track and analyze, as well as strategies for gaining valuable insights from your Shopify store's data.

23.1 Key Metrics and KPIs to Track:

To gain a comprehensive understanding of your store's performance, it's important to monitor a range of metrics and KPIs. Consider the following:

a) Sales and Revenue:

Track your total sales revenue, average order value, and conversion rate to assess the overall financial performance of your store.

b) Traffic and Acquisition:

Monitor the number of visitors to your store, traffic sources, and the effectiveness of your marketing channels to understand how customers are finding your store.

c) Customer Behavior:

Analyze metrics such as bounce rate, time on site, and pages per session to understand how engaged visitors are with your store and identify areas for improvement.

d) Conversion Funnel:

Evaluate the performance of each stage of your conversion funnel, including add-to-cart rate, checkout abandonment rate, and successful order completion rate.

e) Customer Lifetime Value (CLV):

Calculate the average CLV to understand the long-term value of your customers and make informed decisions regarding customer acquisition and retention strategies.

f) Return on Investment (ROI):

Measure the ROI of your marketing campaigns and advertising efforts to assess their effectiveness and allocate resources accordingly.

23.2 Analyzing Store Metrics and KPIs:

To gain valuable insights from your store's data, consider the following strategies:

a) Data Visualization:

Utilize data visualization tools or Shopify's built-in analytics features to transform raw data into clear and visually appealing charts, graphs, and dashboards. This makes it easier to identify trends, patterns, and anomalies.

b) Comparative Analysis:

Compare your store's performance over time by tracking metrics on a regular basis. Identify trends and correlations to understand the impact of changes and marketing initiatives.

c) Segmentation:

Segment your data based on various criteria such as customer demographics, traffic sources, or product categories. This allows you to analyze performance specific to different customer segments and tailor your strategies accordingly.

d) Cohort Analysis:

Perform cohort analysis to track the behavior and purchasing patterns of specific groups of customers over time. This helps you understand customer retention, repeat purchases, and the impact of marketing campaigns.

e) A/B Testing Insights:

Analyze the results of your A/B tests to gain insights into customer preferences, behavior, and the effectiveness of different variations. Use these insights to optimize your store's performance.

23.3 Utilizing Analytics Tools:

Shopify offers built-in analytics tools, but you can also integrate third-party analytics tools to gain deeper insights into your store's performance. Some popular analytics tools include Google Analytics, Kissmetrics, and Mixpanel.

23.4 Taking Action on Insights:

The purpose of analyzing your store's metrics and KPIs is to identify areas for improvement and make data-driven decisions. Once you have gained valuable insights, take action by implementing changes, optimizing marketing campaigns, or adjusting your store's design and user experience.

Conclusion:

Analyzing your Shopify store's metrics and KPIs is vital for understanding your store's performance, identifying areas for improvement, and making data-driven decisions. Track and analyze key metrics related to sales, traffic, customer behavior, and ROI. Utilize data visualization, comparative analysis, segmentation, cohort analysis, and insights from A/B testing to gain valuable insights. Make use of analytics tools to deepen your understanding of store performance. Finally, take action on the insights gained to optimize your store and drive better results.

Chapter 24: Understanding the Basics of SEO for E-Commerce

Search engine optimization (SEO) is essential for improving the visibility and organic traffic of your Shopify e-commerce store. By optimizing your website for search engines, you can increase your chances of ranking higher in search results and attracting relevant, organic traffic. In this chapter, we will explore the basics of SEO for e-commerce and provide strategies to help you improve your Shopify store's search engine visibility.

24.1 The Importance of SEO for E-Commerce:

SEO helps your store appear in search engine results when users search for relevant keywords and phrases related to your products or industry. By optimizing your store for SEO, you can:

a) Increase Organic Traffic:

Improve your store's visibility in search results, leading to increased organic traffic from users actively searching for products or information.

b) Enhance User Experience:

Implementing SEO best practices often aligns with creating a better user experience on your store, including faster loading times, mobile-friendliness, and user-friendly navigation.

c) Boost Conversions:

When your store ranks higher in search results, it gains credibility and trust, resulting in higher click-through rates and improved conversion rates.

24.2 Keyword Research:

Keyword research is the foundation of SEO. It involves identifying the keywords and phrases that users are searching for to find products similar to yours. Consider the following strategies:

a) Relevant Keywords:

Identify keywords that are highly relevant to your products and target audience. Use tools like Google Keyword Planner, SEMrush, or Moz Keyword Explorer to discover popular and relevant keywords.

b) Long-Tail Keywords:

Focus on long-tail keywords, which are more specific and less competitive than generic keywords. Long-tail keywords often have higher conversion rates as they align with users' specific search intent.

c) Competitive Analysis:

Analyze the keywords used by your competitors to gain insights and discover potential keyword opportunities. Look for gaps or underserved areas in the market that you can target.

24.3 On-Page Optimization:

Optimizing your on-page elements is crucial for search engine visibility. Consider the following on-page optimization strategies:

a) Title Tags and Meta Descriptions:

Craft compelling and keyword-rich title tags and meta descriptions for each page of your Shopify store. These elements appear in search results and influence click-through rates.

b) URL Structure:

Ensure your URLs are clean, descriptive, and include relevant keywords. Use hyphens to separate words and keep URLs concise and user-friendly.

c) Heading Tags:

Use heading tags (H1, H2, etc.) to structure your content and make it easier for search engines to understand the hierarchy and importance of your headings.

d) Optimized Product Descriptions:

Write unique and keyword-optimized product descriptions that provide valuable information to both search engines and users. Include relevant keywords naturally and avoid keyword stuffing.

24.4 Technical SEO:

Technical SEO involves optimizing the technical aspects of your store for search engines. Consider the following technical SEO strategies:

a) Website Speed:

Optimize your store's loading speed by compressing images, minifying code, and leveraging caching techniques. A fast-loading website improves user experience and search engine rankings.

b) Mobile-Friendliness:

Ensure your Shopify store is fully responsive and mobile-friendly. With the increasing use of mobile devices, mobile optimization is crucial for SEO and user experience.

c) XML Sitemap:

Create and submit an XML sitemap to search engines, which helps them discover and index your store's pages more effectively.

d) Schema Markup:

Implement schema markup to provide search engines with structured data about your products, such as price, availability, and reviews. This can enhance your store's visibility in search results.

24.5 Content Strategy:

Develop a comprehensive content strategy that incorporates SEO. Consider the following content optimization strategies:

a) Blogging:

Publish informative and engaging blog posts related to your products, industry, or customer interests. Optimize your blog content with relevant keywords and internal links to your product pages.

b) User-Generated Content:

Encourage customers to leave reviews and testimonials on your product pages. User-generated content adds credibility and enhances your store's visibility in search results.

c) Link Building:

Build high-quality backlinks to your store from authoritative websites. Seek opportunities for guest blogging, influencer collaborations, and partnerships to earn valuable inbound links.

24.6 Monitoring and Measurement:

Regularly monitor and measure the effectiveness of your SEO efforts. Utilize analytics tools like Google Analytics to track organic traffic, keyword rankings, and user engagement metrics.

Conclusion:

Understanding the basics of SEO for e-commerce is essential for improving your Shopify store's search engine visibility and attracting organic traffic. Conduct thorough keyword research, optimize on-page elements, address technical SEO aspects, and develop a content strategy aligned with SEO best practices. Regularly monitor and measure your SEO efforts to make informed optimizations.

Chapter 25: Leveraging Paid Advertising on Google and Facebook to Drive Traffic and Sales

Paid advertising on platforms like Google and Facebook can be a highly effective strategy for driving targeted traffic and generating sales for your Shopify store. In this chapter, we will explore the fundamentals of leveraging paid advertising on these platforms, including Google Ads and Facebook Ads, to maximize your store's visibility, reach your target audience, and boost sales.

25.1 Understanding Google Ads:

Google Ads allows you to create and display ads on Google's search engine results pages (SERPs), partner websites, and YouTube. Consider the following strategies for leveraging Google Ads:

a) Keyword Research:

Conduct thorough keyword research to identify relevant and high-performing keywords that align with your products and target audience. Utilize tools like Google Keyword Planner or SEMrush to discover keyword opportunities.

b) Campaign Structure:

Organize your campaigns into relevant ad groups based on product categories or themes. This allows for better targeting and customization of your ads.

c) Ad Formats:

Utilize different ad formats such as text ads, shopping ads, or display ads, depending on your campaign goals and target audience. Create compelling ad copy that includes relevant keywords and strong calls-to-action.

d) Landing Pages:

Ensure that your ad links direct users to optimized landing pages on your Shopify store. The landing pages should be relevant to the ad and provide a seamless user experience, leading to conversions.

e) Tracking and Analytics:

Implement conversion tracking and utilize Google Analytics to measure the performance of your Google Ads campaigns. Track important metrics such as click-through rate (CTR), conversion rate, and return on ad spend (ROAS) to optimize your campaigns.

25.2 Harnessing the Power of Facebook Ads:

Facebook Ads allows you to reach a wide audience based on demographics, interests, and behaviors. Consider the following strategies for leveraging Facebook Ads:

a) Audience Targeting:

Utilize Facebook's targeting options to reach your ideal audience. Define your target audience based on demographics, interests, and behaviors that align with your products. Refine your targeting over time based on performance data.

b) Ad Creatives:

Create visually appealing and engaging ad creatives that resonate with your target audience. Use compelling images or videos, along with persuasive ad copy, to capture attention and drive clicks.

c) Custom Audiences:

Leverage custom audiences on Facebook by retargeting website visitors, email subscribers, or existing customers. Custom audiences allow you to reach users who have already shown interest in your products, increasing the likelihood of conversions.

d) Lookalike Audiences:

Create lookalike audiences based on your existing customer base to find new, similar users who are likely to be interested in your products. Lookalike audiences expand your reach to potential customers with similar characteristics and behaviors.

e) Ad Testing and Optimization:

Regularly test different ad variations, targeting options, and ad placements to optimize your Facebook Ads campaigns. Monitor performance metrics such as click-through rate, conversion rate, and cost per acquisition (CPA) to identify winning combinations.

25.3 Budgeting and Optimization:

To make the most of your paid advertising campaigns, consider the following budgeting and optimization strategies:

a) Budget Allocation:

Allocate your advertising budget based on the platforms and campaigns that are driving the best results for your store. Regularly evaluate and adjust your budget to maximize ROI.

b) A/B Testing:

Conduct A/B testing to compare different ad variations, targeting options, or landing page designs. Test one element at a time and measure the impact on performance metrics to make data-driven optimizations.

c) Ad Performance Analysis:

Analyze the performance of your ads regularly to identify trends, patterns, and opportunities for improvement. Make data-driven decisions to optimize your campaigns and allocate resources effectively.

d) Retargeting:

Implement retargeting campaigns to reach users who have previously visited your store but did not convert. By reminding them of your products, you can increase the likelihood of conversions and repeat visits.

25.4 Ad Policy Compliance and Ad Quality:

Ensure your ads comply with the policies of the advertising platforms to avoid any disruptions or penalties. Create high-quality, relevant, and engaging ads that provide value to the users.

Conclusion:

Paid advertising on Google and Facebook can be a powerful strategy for driving targeted traffic and generating sales for your Shopify store. By understanding the fundamentals of Google Ads and Facebook Ads, conducting thorough audience targeting, optimizing your ad creatives, and continuously monitoring and optimizing your campaigns, you can maximize the effectiveness of your paid advertising efforts.

Chapter 26: Building a Referral Marketing Program to Boost Sales

Referral marketing is a powerful strategy for growing your Shopify store by leveraging the influence and recommendations of your satisfied customers. By encouraging and incentivizing your existing customers to refer their friends and family to your store, you can tap into a network of potential customers who are more likely to convert. In this chapter, we will explore the process of building a referral marketing program to boost sales and expand your customer base.

26.1 The Benefits of Referral Marketing:

Referral marketing offers several benefits for your Shopify store, including:

a) Increased Customer Trust:

Referrals from friends and family are highly trusted by potential customers, making them more likely to make a purchase from your store.

b) Expanded Reach:

Referrals enable you to reach new audiences and tap into networks that may not have been accessible through other marketing channels.

c) Higher Conversion Rates:

Referred customers tend to have higher conversion rates and lifetime value compared to other customer acquisition channels.

d) Cost-Effectiveness:

Referral marketing can be a cost-effective strategy as it leverages existing customers' advocacy rather than relying solely on paid advertising.

26.2 Setting Clear Program Objectives:

Before implementing a referral marketing program, define your objectives to align with your store's goals. Consider the following objectives:

a) New Customer Acquisition:

Focus on acquiring new customers through referrals to expand your customer base.

b) Repeat Purchases:

Encourage referrals from existing customers to drive repeat purchases and customer loyalty.

c) Increased Sales:

Design your referral program to boost overall sales by incentivizing customers to refer others who are likely to convert.

26.3 Designing an Effective Referral Program:

To build a successful referral marketing program, consider the following steps:

a) Define Referral Incentives:

Determine the incentives you will offer to both the referrer and the referred customer. Common incentives include discounts, store credits, free products, or exclusive access to promotions.

b) Establish Program Structure:

Decide on the structure of your referral program. Will it be a one-time incentive for each successful referral, or will it include tiers or levels for additional rewards? Set clear rules and guidelines for participation.

c) Create Referral Tracking Mechanisms:

Implement tracking mechanisms to ensure accurate attribution of referrals. Use unique referral codes or links for each referrer to track conversions and reward them accordingly.

d) Promote and Communicate:

Promote your referral program through various channels, including email marketing, social media, website banners, and personalized messages. Clearly communicate the program's benefits and how customers can participate.

26.4 Nurturing Referral Relationships:

To maximize the effectiveness of your referral program, consider the following strategies:

a) Provide Exceptional Customer Experiences:

Ensure your customers have a positive experience with your store by delivering exceptional customer service, quality products, and seamless shopping experiences. Satisfied customers are more likely to refer others.

b) Personalize Referral Requests:

When requesting referrals, personalize your communication and emphasize the value the referrer and the referred customer will receive. Make it easy for customers to share their referral links or codes.

c) Follow-Up and Reward Promptly:

When a referral results in a conversion, promptly reward the referrer and thank them for their contribution. Show appreciation for their advocacy and maintain a positive relationship.

26.5 Monitoring and Optimization:

Continuously monitor the performance of your referral marketing program and make necessary optimizations:

a) Track Referral Metrics:

Measure the success of your program by tracking metrics such as referral conversion rate, revenue generated from referrals, and the lifetime value of referred customers.

b) Test and Iterate:

Experiment with different incentives, program structures, and promotional strategies. Test different messaging and referral channels to optimize your program's performance.

c) Encourage Feedback:

Collect feedback from participants to gain insights into their experience with the referral program. Use the feedback to identify areas for improvement and make necessary adjustments.

Conclusion:

A well-designed referral marketing program can be a powerful tool for boosting sales and expanding your customer base. By incentivizing and empowering your existing customers to refer others to your Shopify store, you can tap into the power of word-of-mouth marketing. Define clear program objectives, design an effective referral program, nurture referral relationships, and continuously monitor and optimize your program for maximum impact.

Chapter 27: Crafting Effective Product Bundles and Cross-Sell/Up-Sell Strategies

Product bundles and cross-sell/up-sell strategies are valuable techniques for increasing average order value, maximizing customer satisfaction, and driving repeat purchases on your Shopify store. By offering complementary products or enticing customers to upgrade their purchases, you can increase revenue and enhance the overall shopping experience. In this chapter, we will explore the process of crafting effective product bundles and implementing cross-sell/up-sell strategies to boost sales and customer satisfaction.

27.1 Understanding the Benefits of Product Bundles:

Product bundles refer to the packaging of multiple products together as a single offering. Consider the following benefits of product bundles:

a) Increased Perceived Value:

By bundling related products at a discounted price, customers perceive greater value compared to purchasing individual items separately.

b) Higher Average Order Value:

Product bundles encourage customers to spend more by incentivizing them to purchase additional items that complement their original purchase.

c) Cross-Promotion:

Bundling products allows you to cross-promote different items within your inventory, increasing exposure and sales for all included products.

d) Inventory Management:

Bundling slower-moving products with popular items can help manage inventory and increase sales velocity.

27.2 Crafting Effective Product Bundles:

To create compelling product bundles, consider the following strategies:

a) Understand Customer Preferences:

Analyze customer purchase history, behavior, and preferences to identify products that are frequently purchased together. This data-driven approach ensures that your bundles align with customer preferences.

b) Complementary Products:

Select products that naturally complement each other and offer enhanced value when used together. For example, bundling a camera with a lens, tripod, and memory card.

c) Tiered Bundles:

Create different tiers of bundles to cater to various customer segments and budgets. Offering both basic and premium bundles allows customers to choose the option that best suits their needs.

d) Exclusive Bundles:

Create exclusive bundles that are only available through your store. This adds a sense of exclusivity and encourages customers to make the purchase directly from your Shopify store.

e) Clear Messaging and Savings Highlight:

Communicate the benefits and savings of purchasing the bundle upfront. Use clear messaging, attractive visuals, and emphasize the discounted price to entice customers.

27.3 Implementing Cross-Sell/Up-Sell Strategies:

Cross-selling and up-selling techniques encourage customers to purchase additional or upgraded products. Consider the following strategies:

a) Product Recommendations:

Leverage customer data, such as purchase history and browsing behavior, to provide personalized product recommendations on product pages or during the checkout process.

b) Complementary Add-Ons:

Offer complementary add-ons or accessories that enhance the functionality or enjoyment of the main product. For example, suggesting a protective case for a smartphone.

c) Upgrade Options:

Present customers with upgrade options that provide additional features, improved quality, or enhanced performance. Clearly communicate the value and benefits of the upgraded product.

d) Bundled Savings:

Incentivize customers to upgrade or add on products by offering bundle discounts or exclusive offers for purchasing multiple items together.

27.4 Testing and Optimization:

Continuously test and optimize your product bundles and cross-sell/up-sell strategies to maximize their effectiveness:

a) A/B Testing:

Test different bundle combinations, pricing strategies, and cross-sell/up-sell placements to determine which options yield the highest conversion rates and revenue.

b) Monitoring Customer Feedback:

Pay attention to customer feedback and reviews to understand how customers perceive your bundles and cross-sell/up-sell offers. Use the feedback to make improvements and address any concerns.

c) Analytics and Performance Tracking:

Monitor key metrics such as average order value, conversion rates, and revenue generated from product bundles and cross-sell/up-sell strategies. Use this data to identify trends and make data-driven optimizations.

Conclusion:

Crafting effective product bundles and implementing cross-sell/up-sell strategies can significantly impact your Shopify store's revenue and customer satisfaction. By understanding customer preferences, selecting complementary products, and using persuasive messaging, you can create enticing bundles that drive higher average order values. Additionally, by offering relevant product recommendations and upgrade options, you can encourage customers to make additional purchases or upgrade their selections. Continuously test, optimize, and monitor the performance of your bundles and cross-sell/up-sell strategies to ensure their effectiveness.

Chapter 28: Creating a Loyalty Program to Encourage Repeat Purchases

A loyalty program is a powerful tool for fostering customer loyalty, encouraging repeat purchases, and driving customer engagement on your Shopify store. By rewarding and incentivizing your customers for their ongoing support and purchases, you can build long-term relationships and increase customer lifetime value. In this chapter, we will explore the process of creating an effective loyalty program to encourage repeat purchases and enhance customer loyalty.

28.1 Understanding the Benefits of a Loyalty Program:

Implementing a loyalty program on your Shopify store offers several benefits, including:

a) Repeat Purchases:

A well-designed loyalty program incentivizes customers to return to your store for future purchases, increasing their lifetime value and overall revenue.

b) Customer Retention:

By rewarding customers for their loyalty, you create a strong bond and encourage them to continue choosing your store over competitors.

c) Increased Engagement:

Loyalty programs provide opportunities for increased engagement, such as exclusive offers, personalized recommendations, and early access to new products or promotions.

d) Word-of-Mouth Marketing:

Satisfied and loyal customers are more likely to refer your store to friends and family, amplifying your brand's reach through positive word-of-mouth.

28.2 Designing Your Loyalty Program:

To create an effective loyalty program, consider the following steps:

a) Define Program Objectives:

Establish clear objectives for your loyalty program, such as increasing customer retention, boosting average order value, or driving customer referrals. Align your program with your store's overall goals.

b) Determine Rewards Structure:

Decide on the types of rewards you will offer, such as discounts, store credits, free products, exclusive access to promotions, or VIP perks. Consider the value and attainability of the rewards to ensure they are compelling to your customers.

c) Establish Point System or Tiered Program:

Choose whether to implement a point-based system where customers earn points for each purchase, or a tiered program where customers unlock higher levels of rewards based on their loyalty. Tailor the structure to fit your customer base and business model.

d) Personalize Rewards:

Segment your customer base and personalize rewards based on customer preferences and purchase history. This customization enhances the customer experience and increases the perceived value of the rewards.

e) Program Accessibility:

Ensure your loyalty program is easy to understand, join, and participate in. Streamline the sign-up process and clearly communicate the benefits of the program to customers.

28.3 Promoting Your Loyalty Program:

To maximize participation in your loyalty program, employ the following strategies:

a) Multi-Channel Promotion:

Promote your loyalty program across various channels, including your website, email marketing campaigns, social media platforms, and in-store signage (if applicable). Consistently communicate the benefits and encourage sign-ups.

b) Exclusive Offers:

Provide exclusive offers or discounts to loyalty program members to incentivize sign-ups and reward their ongoing loyalty.

c) Referral Incentives:

Encourage existing loyalty program members to refer friends and family to join the program by offering additional rewards or bonuses for successful referrals.

d) Communication and Engagement:

Regularly communicate with your loyalty program members, updating them on their rewards balance, upcoming promotions, and exclusive events. Foster engagement through personalized emails and targeted offers.

28.4 Monitoring and Optimization:

Continuously monitor and optimize your loyalty program to ensure its effectiveness:

a) Track Key Metrics:

Monitor key metrics such as member sign-ups, redemption rates, customer retention, and the impact on overall sales. Analyze the data to identify trends and areas for improvement.

b) Collect Customer Feedback:

Solicit feedback from loyalty program members to understand their experience and satisfaction levels. Use their insights to make necessary adjustments and improve the program.

c) Test and Iterate:

Experiment with different reward structures, promotional strategies, and communication tactics to optimize the program's performance. A/B testing can help identify the most effective approaches.

Conclusion:

Implementing a well-designed loyalty program can significantly impact customer retention, repeat purchases, and overall customer satisfaction on your Shopify store. By defining program objectives, designing compelling rewards, and effectively promoting the program, you can foster long-term customer loyalty. Continuously monitor the program's performance, collect customer feedback, and make data-driven optimizations to ensure its success.

Chapter 29: Managing Your Inventory and Fulfillment Process

Efficient inventory management and a streamlined fulfillment process are crucial for running a successful e-commerce business on Shopify. By effectively managing your inventory levels, optimizing order fulfillment, and ensuring timely delivery, you can provide a seamless customer experience and maintain a healthy supply chain. In this chapter, we will explore strategies for managing your inventory and streamlining your fulfillment process to meet customer expectations and drive business growth.

29.1 Inventory Management:

a) Accurate Inventory Tracking:

Implement an inventory management system that allows you to accurately track your inventory levels in real-time. This helps prevent stockouts, avoid overstocking, and ensure the availability of popular products.

b) Demand Forecasting:

Utilize historical sales data, market trends, and customer insights to forecast demand for your products. This allows you to make informed decisions about inventory replenishment and avoid stock imbalances.

c) Stock Reordering:

Set up automatic reorder points for your products to trigger replenishment orders when inventory levels reach a certain threshold. This helps maintain optimal inventory levels and minimizes the risk of running out of stock.

d) Inventory Optimization:

Regularly review your product assortment and identify slow-moving or obsolete inventory. Consider discounting or liquidating these items to free up storage space and allocate resources to more profitable products.

29.2 Order Fulfillment:

a) Efficient Order Processing:

Streamline your order processing workflow by automating repetitive tasks, such as order confirmation emails, picking lists, and shipping labels. This reduces errors and speeds up the fulfillment process.

b) Warehouse Organization:

Optimize your warehouse layout to minimize the time and effort required to locate and pick items for orders. Categorize products logically, use bin locations, and regularly organize and clean the warehouse space.

c) Shipping Integration:

Integrate your Shopify store with shipping carriers or fulfillment services to streamline the shipping process. Automatically generate shipping labels, track packages, and provide customers with shipment notifications.

d)Packaging and Branding:

Invest in high-quality packaging materials that protect your products during transit and align with your brand image. Consider including branded inserts or personalized thank-you notes to enhance the customer experience.

29.3 Timely Delivery:

a) Shipping Time Estimates:

Clearly communicate shipping time estimates on your product pages and during the checkout process. Set realistic expectations and ensure your chosen shipping methods can meet those deadlines.

b) Expedited Shipping Options:

Offer expedited shipping options for customers who require faster delivery. Calculate the additional cost accurately and provide transparent delivery timelines for each option.

c) Order Tracking:

Provide customers with tracking information for their orders so they can monitor the progress and estimated delivery date. This reduces anxiety and improves overall customer satisfaction.

d) Customer Communication:

Proactively communicate with customers regarding any potential delays, backorders, or shipping issues. Promptly address their concerns and provide alternative solutions whenever possible.

29.4 Continuous Improvement:

a) Data Analysis:

Regularly analyze inventory and fulfillment data to identify bottlenecks, areas for improvement, and opportunities to optimize processes. Leverage analytics tools and key performance indicators (KPIs) to monitor your inventory and fulfillment performance.

b) Supplier Collaboration:

Maintain strong relationships with your suppliers and engage in open communication. Collaborate on forecasting, lead times, and potential supply chain disruptions to mitigate risks and ensure a smooth inventory replenishment process.

c) Customer Feedback:

Listen to customer feedback regarding the fulfillment process. Pay attention to any complaints or suggestions and use this valuable information to make necessary adjustments and improvements.

Conclusion:

Effective inventory management and a streamlined fulfillment process are critical for running a successful e-commerce business on Shopify. By accurately tracking inventory, forecasting demand, optimizing order fulfillment, and ensuring timely delivery, you can provide a seamless customer experience and drive business growth.

Continuously analyze data, seek supplier collaboration, and listen to customer feedback to identify areas for improvement and make informed decisions.

Chapter 30: Building a Customer Service Team to Provide Top-Notch Support

Providing exceptional customer service is crucial for the success of your e-commerce business on Shopify. A dedicated customer service team can help build trust, enhance customer satisfaction, and foster long-term loyalty. In this chapter, we will discuss strategies for building an effective customer service team that delivers top-notch support to your customers.

30.1 Understanding the Importance of Customer Service:

a) Customer Satisfaction:

Exceptional customer service ensures that your customers are satisfied with their overall shopping experience. It helps address their concerns, resolve issues promptly, and exceed their expectations.

b) Reputation and Brand Image:

Positive customer experiences and excellent service contribute to a strong brand reputation and positive word-of-mouth marketing. Happy customers are more likely to recommend your store to others.

c) Repeat Purchases and Customer Loyalty:

When customers receive excellent support, they are more likely to become repeat customers and develop loyalty towards your brand. A satisfied customer is more likely to trust your business and choose you over competitors.

30.2 Building Your Customer Service Team:

a) Define Roles and Responsibilities:

Determine the specific roles and responsibilities within your customer service team. These may include customer support agents, team leads, supervisors, and managers. Clearly define their tasks and areas of expertise.

b) Hiring the Right Team Members:

Look for individuals who possess strong communication skills, empathy, problem-solving abilities, and a customer-centric mindset. Prioritize candidates who have experience in customer service roles or demonstrate a genuine passion for helping others.

c) Training and Development:

Invest in training programs to equip your customer service team with the necessary skills and knowledge. Train them on your products, policies, and procedures, as well as effective communication and conflict resolution techniques.

d) Team Collaboration and Support:

Encourage a collaborative and supportive team environment. Foster open communication channels, provide opportunities for feedback and idea sharing, and promote a positive and inclusive work culture.

30.3 Implementing Effective Customer Service Practices:

a) Prompt Response Times:

Set clear expectations for response times and ensure your team is equipped to handle customer inquiries in a timely manner. Utilize help desk software or ticketing systems to track and manage customer inquiries efficiently.

b) Multichannel Support:

Offer customer support across multiple channels, such as email, live chat, phone, and social media. Be present and responsive on the channels preferred by your customers to provide a seamless and convenient support experience.

c) Personalized Assistance:

Train your team to provide personalized and empathetic assistance to customers. Encourage active listening, address customers by name, and tailor responses to their specific needs and concerns.

d) Problem Resolution:

Empower your customer service team to effectively resolve customer issues and complaints. Provide them with clear guidelines and authority to make decisions that prioritize customer satisfaction.

30.4 Continuous Improvement and Feedback:

a) Customer Feedback:

Encourage customers to provide feedback on their support experiences. Collect and analyze this feedback to identify areas for improvement and make necessary adjustments to your customer service processes.

b) Team Training and Development:

Continuously invest in the training and development of your customer service team. Offer ongoing training sessions, workshops, and resources to enhance their skills and knowledge.

c) Performance Evaluation:

Regularly evaluate the performance of your customer service team. Use key performance indicators (KPIs) such as customer satisfaction ratings, response times, and issue resolution rates to assess individual and team performance.

Conclusion:

Building a customer service team that provides top-notch support is essential for the success of your Shopify store. By hiring the right team members, providing comprehensive training, implementing effective customer service practices, and continuously seeking feedback and improvement, you can deliver exceptional customer experiences that build trust and loyalty.

Chapter 31: Handling Returns and Refunds Efficiently and Professionally

Dealing with returns and refunds is an integral part of running an e-commerce business on Shopify. Efficiently and professionally managing the return process is crucial for customer satisfaction and maintaining a positive brand image. In this chapter, we will discuss strategies for handling returns and refunds in a manner that is both efficient for your business and satisfying for your customers.

31.1 Importance of a Smooth Returns Process:

a) Customer Satisfaction:

A hassle-free and customer-centric returns process demonstrates your commitment to customer satisfaction. It reassures customers that they can shop with confidence, knowing they have the option to return or exchange products if needed.

b) Brand Reputation:

Efficiently handling returns and refunds contributes to a positive brand reputation. Customers are more likely to trust and recommend a business that demonstrates fairness, transparency, and a commitment to resolving issues.

c) Repeat Purchases and Customer Loyalty:

By providing a seamless returns experience, you can enhance customer loyalty. Satisfied customers are more likely to make repeat purchases and continue their relationship with your brand.

31.2 Creating a Clear and Fair Returns Policy:

a) Clearly Communicate the Policy:

Ensure that your returns policy is clearly stated on your website, including details such as the time frame for returns, acceptable conditions for returns, and any associated fees or requirements. Make it easily accessible and visible to customers.

b) Fair and Reasonable Terms:

Craft a returns policy that balances customer satisfaction with your business's operational needs. Consider factors such as return windows, acceptable reasons for returns, and guidelines for returning different types of products.

c) Flexibility and Exceptions:

Acknowledge that there may be unique situations where exceptions to the returns policy are warranted. Train your customer service team to handle such cases with empathy and a focus on finding fair resolutions.

31.3 Streamlining the Returns Process:

a) Simplify the Return Request Process:

Provide customers with a user-friendly and straightforward return request process. Utilize an online portal or a dedicated email address where customers can initiate return requests, providing all necessary details.

b) Automate Return Labels:

Consider integrating your Shopify store with a shipping carrier or fulfillment service that allows for automated return labels. This simplifies the return shipping process for both you and your customers.

c) Provide Prepaid Return Labels:

Offer prepaid return labels, especially for cases where the return is due to product defects or errors on your end. This helps alleviate customer concerns about return shipping costs and adds to their overall satisfaction.

d) Track Return Shipments:

Implement a system to track return shipments to ensure they are received and processed promptly. This allows you to keep customers informed about the status of their returns and enables you to take appropriate actions.

31.4 Efficient Refund Processing:

a) Prompt Refund Initiation:

Initiate refunds promptly upon receiving the returned products or confirmation of return shipment. Clearly communicate the expected timeframe for the refund to be processed.

b) Secure Payment Reversals:

Ensure that the refund process is secure and accurate. Reverse the payment through the same method used for the original transaction (e.g., credit card refund, PayPal refund) to maintain transparency and avoid complications.

c) Notify Customers of Refund Completion:

Notify customers once their refund has been processed, providing them with confirmation and any relevant details. This helps build trust and keeps customers informed about the status of their return.

31.5 Continuous Improvement and Analysis:

a) Analyze Return Data:

Regularly analyze return data to identify patterns, common reasons for returns, and potential areas for improvement. Use this information to make data-driven decisions to reduce return rates and enhance product quality.

b) Customer Feedback and Insights:

Seek customer feedback regarding their returns experience. Leverage this feedback to improve the returns process, identify pain points, and address any customer concerns or suggestions.

c) Supplier Collaboration:

Collaborate with suppliers to address recurring product issues leading to returns. Work closely with them to improve product quality, packaging, and shipping processes, ultimately reducing return rates.

Conclusion:

Efficiently and professionally handling returns and refunds is crucial for maintaining customer satisfaction and a positive brand image. By creating a clear returns policy, streamlining the returns process, processing refunds promptly, and continuously analyzing return data, you can ensure a smooth returns experience for your customers while minimizing the impact on your business operations.

Chapter 32: Scaling Your Shopify Business: When and How to Expand Your Operations

As your Shopify business grows, you may reach a point where expanding your operations becomes necessary. Scaling your business requires careful planning and strategic decision-making to ensure sustained growth and success. In this chapter, we will explore when and how to expand your operations to accommodate increasing demand and take your Shopify business to the next level.

32.1 Signs that It's Time to Scale Your Business:

a) Increased Sales and Demand:

When your sales consistently exceed your current capacity to fulfill orders or meet customer demands, it's a clear sign that scaling your operations is necessary.

b) Limitations in Infrastructure and Resources:

If your current infrastructure, such as inventory management systems, order processing, or customer support, is struggling to keep up with growth, it may be time to consider expansion.

c) Opportunities in the Market:

Identify market trends, new customer segments, or untapped geographical areas that present growth opportunities. Expanding your operations can help you seize these opportunities and increase your market share.

d) Financial Stability:

Ensure your business has the financial stability and resources to support expansion. Assess your cash flow, profitability, and access to capital before embarking on a scaling journey.

32.2 Strategies for Scaling Your Shopify Business:

a) Streamline and Automate Processes:

Identify areas within your business operations that can be streamlined and automated. This can include order fulfillment, inventory management, customer support, and marketing campaigns. Implementing efficient systems and software can help you handle increased volume without sacrificing quality.

b) Expand Product Line or Offerings:

Consider expanding your product line or introducing complementary products or services to cater to a broader customer base. Conduct market research to identify potential gaps or opportunities that align with your brand and target market.

c) Partner with Suppliers and Manufacturers:

Establish strategic partnerships with reliable suppliers and manufacturers to ensure a consistent supply of products as you scale. Negotiate favorable terms and leverage economies of scale to optimize costs and improve profitability.

d) Outsourcing and Hiring:

Evaluate which aspects of your business can be outsourced or delegated to external agencies or freelancers. This can include tasks such as digital marketing, website design, customer support, or fulfillment. Additionally, assess your internal team's capacity and consider hiring additional staff to support increased demands.

e) Upgrade Technology and Infrastructure:

Invest in scalable technology solutions that can handle increased traffic, transactions, and data volume. This may involve upgrading your Shopify plan, improving server infrastructure, or adopting advanced analytics and reporting tools to make informed business decisions.

32.3 Considerations for Geographic Expansion:

a) Market Research:

Conduct thorough market research to assess the potential for expansion into new geographic regions. Evaluate local competition, consumer preferences, cultural differences, and legal requirements to determine if there is a viable market for your products or services.

b) Logistics and Supply Chain:

Evaluate the logistics and supply chain challenges associated with expanding into new locations. Consider factors such as shipping costs, customs regulations, warehousing, and distribution networks to ensure smooth operations.

c) Localization and Marketing:

Tailor your marketing and messaging to resonate with the local audience in new geographic regions. Adapt your website, content, and advertising to reflect regional preferences and cultural nuances, ensuring that your brand message remains consistent.

32.4 Monitoring and Adjusting:

a) Key Performance Indicators (KPIs):

Establish and monitor key performance indicators that align with your scaling goals. This can include metrics such as revenue growth, customer acquisition costs, average order value, or customer lifetime value. Regularly track and analyze these metrics to evaluate the success of your scaling efforts.

b) Agile Decision-Making:

Remain flexible and adaptable as you scale your business. Continuously assess the outcomes of your expansion efforts and make necessary adjustments to optimize operations, marketing strategies, and resource allocation.

c) Customer Feedback and Satisfaction:

Pay close attention to customer feedback and satisfaction throughout the scaling process. Engage with your customers to understand their evolving needs and preferences, and make adjustments accordingly to maintain a positive customer experience.

Conclusion:

Scaling your Shopify business is an exciting phase that requires careful planning and execution. By recognizing the signs that it's time to expand, implementing effective scaling strategies, considering geographic expansion when appropriate, and continuously monitoring and adjusting your operations, you can successfully navigate the challenges and take your business to new heights.

Chapter 33: Finding and Hiring Talented Employees to Grow Your Business

As your Shopify business expands, you will likely need to hire talented employees to support your growing operations. Hiring the right people is crucial for the success and continued growth of your business. In this chapter, we will explore strategies for finding and hiring talented employees who can contribute to your business's growth and help you achieve your goals.

33.1 Defining Your Hiring Needs:

a) Assess Your Business Requirements:

Evaluate your current and future business needs to identify the roles and skills required to support your growth. Determine which areas of your business would benefit most from additional talent and expertise.

b) Create Job Descriptions:

Develop clear and concise job descriptions that outline the responsibilities, qualifications, and expectations for each role. Clearly define the skills, experience, and cultural fit you are seeking in potential candidates.

c) Consider Growth Potential:

Look for candidates who not only meet the immediate requirements but also have the potential to grow and take on additional responsibilities as your business expands. Consider their willingness to learn, adapt, and contribute to your long-term vision.

33.2 Sourcing Talent:

a) Internal Referrals:

Tap into your existing network, including current employees, partners, and industry connections, to seek referrals. Encourage your team members to refer qualified candidates who align with your company culture and values.

b) Online Job Platforms:

Utilize online job platforms and professional networking sites to advertise your job openings. Platforms such as LinkedIn, Indeed, and specialized job boards can help you reach a wide pool of candidates actively seeking employment.

c) Attend Industry Events and Job Fairs:

Participate in industry events, conferences, and job fairs to connect with potential candidates directly. These events offer an opportunity to meet individuals who are passionate about your industry and may be seeking new career opportunities.

d) Social Media and Online Presence:

Leverage your company's social media channels and online presence to promote job openings and attract talent. Share compelling content about your company culture, values, and growth opportunities to pique the interest of potential candidates.

33.3 Evaluating Candidates:

a) Review Resumes and Applications:

Thoroughly review resumes and applications to assess candidates' qualifications and experience. Look for relevant skills, achievements, and a demonstrated passion for your industry or field.

b) Conduct Interviews:

Interview candidates to evaluate their fit with your company culture, assess their communication and problem-solving skills, and gain a deeper understanding of their qualifications. Utilize a mix of behavioral and situational questions to gauge their abilities and alignment with your business.

c) Skills Assessments and Tests:

Consider conducting skills assessments or tests to evaluate candidates' abilities in specific areas relevant to their roles. This can provide valuable insights into their technical proficiency and problem-solving capabilities.

d) Reference Checks:

Reach out to references provided by candidates to gather additional insights about their work ethic, teamwork skills, and performance in previous roles. This can help validate their qualifications and suitability for the position.

33.4 Onboarding and Retention:

a) Provide Comprehensive Onboarding:

Develop a structured onboarding program to help new hires quickly understand your company's values, processes, and expectations. Assign a mentor or buddy to support their transition and ensure they feel welcome and supported.

b) Offer Growth and Development Opportunities:

Create a supportive and growth-oriented environment that encourages employees to enhance their skills and advance their careers. Provide training, mentorship programs, and opportunities for professional development to foster their long-term engagement and loyalty.

c) Competitive Compensation and Benefits:

Offer competitive compensation packages and benefits to attract and retain top talent. Consider market trends and industry benchmarks to ensure your offers are competitive and reflective of the value your employees bring to the organization.

d) Foster a Positive Company Culture:

Nurture a positive company culture that values collaboration, transparency, and open communication. Encourage teamwork, recognize achievements, and provide regular feedback to foster employee engagement and satisfaction.

Conclusion:

Finding and hiring talented employees is a critical step in growing your Shopify business. By defining your hiring needs, sourcing talent through various channels, evaluating candidates effectively, and providing a supportive onboarding and retention process, you can build a strong team that drives your business's success.

Chapter 34: Managing Cash Flow and Financial Planning for Your E-Commerce Business

Managing cash flow and financial planning is essential for the success and sustainability of your e-commerce business. Understanding and effectively managing your finances will enable you to make informed decisions, optimize profitability, and navigate through both challenges and opportunities. In this chapter, we will explore strategies for managing cash flow and implementing financial planning practices specific to your e-commerce business.

34.1 Importance of Cash Flow Management:

a) Cash Flow as the Lifeblood:

Cash flow is the lifeblood of your business, representing the movement of money in and out of your company. It affects your ability to pay suppliers, cover operating expenses, invest in growth initiatives, and maintain a healthy financial position.

b) Forecasting and Planning:

Effective cash flow management involves forecasting and planning your inflows and outflows to ensure you have adequate funds to meet your financial obligations and seize growth opportunities.

c) Mitigating Financial Risks:

Proper cash flow management helps mitigate financial risks, such as running out of cash, accumulating excessive debt, or facing liquidity issues during periods of low sales or unforeseen circumstances.

34.2 Strategies for Managing Cash Flow:

a) Accurate Cash Flow Forecasting:

Develop a robust cash flow forecasting process to project your future cash inflows and outflows. Consider factors such as sales cycles, seasonality, payment terms, and operating expenses. Regularly review and update your forecasts to ensure accuracy.

b) Monitoring and Controlling Expenses:

Monitor and control your expenses to maintain a healthy cash flow. Identify areas where you can reduce costs without compromising the quality of your products or services. Negotiate favorable terms with suppliers and vendors to optimize purchasing and inventory management.

c) Managing Accounts Receivable:

Implement efficient accounts receivable management practices to ensure timely collection of payments from customers. Send timely and accurate invoices, establish clear payment terms, and proactively follow up on overdue payments. Consider offering incentives for early payments or implementing a system for recurring billing.

d) Optimizing Inventory Management:

Maintain optimal inventory levels by closely monitoring sales trends, forecasting demand, and implementing just-in-time inventory practices. Avoid overstocking or understocking, as both can negatively impact your cash flow.

e) Negotiating Payment Terms with Suppliers:

Negotiate favorable payment terms with your suppliers to align with your cash flow cycle. Longer payment terms or discounts for early payments can help manage your cash flow more effectively.

34.3 Financial Planning for E-Commerce Businesses:

a) Budgeting and Profitability Analysis:

Develop a comprehensive budget that includes your revenue projections, operating expenses, marketing costs, and other financial factors. Regularly analyze your profitability and make necessary adjustments to optimize your financial performance.

b) Setting Realistic Financial Goals:

Set realistic financial goals based on your business's growth trajectory and market conditions. Break down your goals into achievable milestones and develop strategies to reach them. Regularly review and assess your progress towards these goals.

c) Contingency Planning:

Develop contingency plans for unexpected events or market fluctuations that may impact your cash flow. Maintain an emergency fund to handle unforeseen expenses or temporary disruptions in your revenue streams.

d) Seek Professional Financial Advice:

Consider seeking guidance from financial professionals, such as accountants or financial advisors, who specialize in e-commerce businesses. They can provide valuable insights and help you navigate complex financial matters.

Conclusion:

Managing cash flow and implementing effective financial planning practices are critical for the success of your e-commerce business. By accurately forecasting cash flow, monitoring and controlling expenses, optimizing inventory management, and setting realistic financial goals, you can ensure the financial health and sustainability of your business.

Chapter 35: Negotiating with Suppliers and Other Business Partners

Negotiating effectively with suppliers and other business partners is a crucial skill for e-commerce entrepreneurs. Successful negotiations can result in favorable terms, cost savings, improved relationships, and increased profitability. In this chapter, we will delve into strategies and techniques to help you negotiate with suppliers and other business partners to achieve mutually beneficial outcomes.

35.1 Preparing for Negotiations:

a) Define Your Objectives:

Clearly define your objectives and desired outcomes before entering into negotiations. Identify the specific terms, pricing, or concessions you are seeking from the supplier or business partner.

b) Research and Gather Information:

Thoroughly research the market, industry trends, and competitive landscape to gather relevant information. Understand the supplier's pricing, products, and terms, as well as their reputation and track record.

c) Assess Your Value Proposition:

Evaluate your value proposition and understand the strengths and unique selling points of your business. Identify the value you bring to the table and how it can be leveraged during negotiations.

d) Set Realistic Targets and Alternatives:

Set realistic targets and establish alternative options in case the negotiations do not yield the desired results. Having backup plans or alternative suppliers can provide leverage and increase your negotiating power.

35.2 Effective Negotiation Techniques:

a) Establish Rapport and Build Relationships:

Create a positive and professional rapport with the supplier or business partner. Develop a relationship based on trust, open communication, and mutual respect. Building rapport can enhance the likelihood of reaching favorable outcomes.

b) Active Listening:

Practice active listening during negotiations. Pay close attention to the other party's concerns, needs, and perspectives. This will allow you to understand their position and tailor your arguments or proposals accordingly.

c) Communicate Clearly and Assertively:

Clearly articulate your expectations, requirements, and proposals. Be assertive in presenting your case while maintaining professionalism and respect. Use persuasive language and provide supporting evidence to strengthen your arguments.

d) Seek Win-Win Solutions:

Strive for win-win outcomes where both parties benefit from the negotiation. Look for creative solutions and compromises that address the interests of both sides. Collaborative problem-solving can strengthen the relationship and pave the way for future partnerships.

e) Leverage Comparative Analysis:

Use comparative analysis to highlight the advantages of your proposal or pricing. Showcase the value you bring compared to competitors or alternative options. Data and evidence-based arguments can be persuasive during negotiations.

35.3 Managing Negotiation Challenges:

a) Overcoming Objections:

Anticipate potential objections from the supplier or business partner and prepare effective responses. Address their concerns, provide clarification, or offer alternative solutions to overcome objections.

b) Negotiating Pricing and Terms:

Negotiate pricing and terms that align with your budget and profitability goals. Explore options such as volume discounts, longer payment terms, or favorable shipping arrangements. Be prepared to justify your pricing requests based on market conditions and the value you offer.

c) Building Long-Term Relationships:

Focus on building long-term relationships with your suppliers and business partners. Nurture the relationship beyond the negotiation stage by maintaining open communication, delivering on your promises, and seeking opportunities for collaboration and growth.

d) Reviewing and Renewing Agreements:

Regularly review your agreements and contracts with suppliers and business partners to ensure they align with your evolving needs and market conditions. When renewing agreements, renegotiate terms if necessary and seek improvements or concessions.

Conclusion:

Effective negotiation with suppliers and other business partners is vital for e-commerce success. By preparing thoroughly, employing effective negotiation techniques, and managing negotiation challenges, you can secure favorable terms, build strong relationships, and drive profitability.

Chapter 36: Building Relationships with Other Entrepreneurs and Business Owners

Building relationships with other entrepreneurs and business owners can be a valuable asset for your e-commerce business. Collaborating, sharing insights, and supporting one another can lead to new opportunities, growth, and a stronger entrepreneurial community. In this chapter, we will explore strategies and approaches to effectively build relationships with other entrepreneurs and business owners.

36.1 Networking Opportunities:

a) Attend Industry Events and Conferences:

Participate in industry events and conferences relevant to your e-commerce niche. These events provide valuable networking opportunities, where you can connect with like-minded entrepreneurs, industry experts, and potential business partners.

b) Join Professional Associations and Communities:

Become a member of professional associations or communities related to e-commerce or your specific niche. These organizations often host networking events, webinars, and forums where you can engage with other entrepreneurs and gain industry insights.

c) Engage in Online Forums and Social Media Groups:

Join online forums and social media groups focused on e-commerce or your niche. Actively participate by sharing your expertise, asking questions, and offering support to fellow entrepreneurs. These platforms can be excellent sources for building connections and fostering meaningful relationships.

36.2 Collaborative Opportunities:

a) Seek Collaboration Projects:

Look for collaboration opportunities with complementary businesses or entrepreneurs. Explore partnerships for joint marketing campaigns, product bundles, or cross-promotions. Collaborative projects can expand your reach, introduce your brand to new audiences, and generate mutually beneficial outcomes.

b) Share Industry Insights and Knowledge:

Be open to sharing your industry insights, experiences, and expertise with other entrepreneurs. Write guest blog posts, contribute to podcasts, or host webinars where you can share valuable knowledge. By providing value to others, you establish yourself as an authority and build credibility within the entrepreneurial community.

c) Participate in Mastermind Groups:

Join or form a mastermind group with other entrepreneurs. These groups provide a platform for sharing ideas, receiving feedback, and receiving support from a trusted circle of peers. Through regular meetings and discussions, you can collectively solve challenges, learn from each other's experiences, and inspire one another.

36.3 Cultivating Relationships:

a) Be Genuine and Authentic:

When interacting with other entrepreneurs, be genuine and authentic in your approach. Show a sincere interest in their businesses and endeavors. Building relationships based on trust and authenticity lays the foundation for long-lasting connections.

b) Be a Supportive Listener:

Practice active listening when engaging in conversations with fellow entrepreneurs. Show genuine interest in their stories, challenges, and successes. Offer support, advice, or resources when appropriate. By being a supportive listener, you build rapport and foster strong relationships.

c) Provide Value and Support:

Look for opportunities to provide value and support to other entrepreneurs. This can range from sharing helpful resources, recommending tools or service providers, or making introductions to potential collaborators. By being a valuable resource to others, you strengthen your position within the entrepreneurial community.

d) Nurture Relationships Over Time:

Building relationships takes time and effort. Regularly follow up with the entrepreneurs you connect with, maintain communication, and find ways to support each other's businesses. Celebrate their milestones and achievements, and be there to offer encouragement during challenging times. Consistency and genuine care help nurture long-term relationships.

Conclusion:

Building relationships with other entrepreneurs and business owners is a powerful strategy for e-commerce success. By actively networking, seeking collaborative opportunities, and cultivating genuine relationships, you can tap into a supportive entrepreneurial community, gain valuable insights, and uncover new possibilities for growth.

Chapter 37: Dealing with Legal and Regulatory Issues that Affect E-Commerce Businesses

Operating an e-commerce business involves navigating various legal and regulatory requirements. Understanding and complying with these obligations is essential to protect your business, build trust with customers, and avoid legal issues. In this chapter, we will explore common legal and regulatory considerations that affect e-commerce businesses and provide guidance on how to address them.

37.1 Understanding E-Commerce Laws and Regulations:

a) Consumer Protection Laws:

Familiarize yourself with consumer protection laws specific to e-commerce, such as regulations governing product descriptions, warranties, refunds, and privacy. Comply with these laws to ensure transparency, fair treatment of customers, and protection against potential legal disputes.

b) Data Protection and Privacy:

Adhere to data protection and privacy regulations, such as the General Data Protection Regulation (GDPR) and the California Consumer Privacy Act (CCPA). Implement measures to secure customer data, obtain proper consent for data collection, and provide clear privacy policies.

c) Intellectual Property Rights:

Respect intellectual property rights, including trademarks, copyrights, and patents. Avoid using copyrighted materials without permission, properly license images and content, and conduct thorough searches to ensure your brand and products do not infringe on existing trademarks.

d) Advertising and Marketing Regulations:

Stay compliant with advertising and marketing regulations, including rules on truth in advertising, disclosure of sponsored content, and email marketing regulations. Understand the guidelines set by platforms like Google and social media networks regarding advertising practices.

37.2 Creating and Reviewing Legal Documentation:

a) Terms and Conditions:

Draft comprehensive terms and conditions that outline the rights and responsibilities of both your business and customers. Include provisions on refunds, warranties, limitations of liability, dispute resolution, and governing law. Regularly review and update these terms to reflect any changes in laws or business practices.

b) Privacy Policy:

Develop a privacy policy that clearly explains how customer data is collected, stored, and used. Include information on data security measures, third-party data sharing, and customer rights regarding their personal information. Ensure your policy is accessible and prominently displayed on your website.

c) Shipping and Returns Policy:

Create a shipping and returns policy that outlines shipping methods, delivery times, return procedures, and any associated fees. Clearly communicate these policies to customers to manage expectations and minimize potential disputes.

d) Dispute Resolution and Arbitration:

Consider including a dispute resolution clause in your terms and conditions, specifying a preferred method of resolving disputes, such as negotiation or arbitration. Understand the pros and cons of different dispute resolution methods and consult legal experts if needed.

37.3 Compliance and Risk Management:

a) Regular Legal Compliance Reviews:

Periodically review your business operations, policies, and documentation to ensure ongoing compliance with relevant laws and regulations. Stay updated on changes in legislation and consult legal professionals when needed to address any compliance gaps.

b) Intellectual Property Protection:

Protect your intellectual property by registering trademarks, copyrights, or patents when applicable. Conduct regular searches to identify potential infringements on your intellectual property and take appropriate action to defend your rights.

c) Risk Management and Insurance:

Assess potential risks associated with your e-commerce business, such as cybersecurity threats, product liability, or data breaches. Obtain appropriate insurance coverage, such as general liability insurance or cyber insurance, to mitigate potential financial losses.

d) Legal Consultation:

When faced with complex legal issues, consult with qualified attorneys who specialize in e-commerce and technology law. Seek their guidance on matters like compliance, intellectual property, contract drafting, and dispute resolution.

Conclusion:

Understanding and addressing legal and regulatory issues is crucial for the success and longevity of your e-commerce business. By staying informed about e-commerce laws and regulations, creating and reviewing necessary legal documentation, and implementing effective compliance and risk management practices, you can navigate the legal landscape confidently and protect your business interests.

Chapter 38: Staying Up-to-Date with the Latest Trends and Innovations in E-Commerce

The e-commerce landscape is constantly evolving, driven by technological advancements, shifting consumer behavior, and emerging trends. To stay competitive and seize new opportunities, it's crucial for e-commerce entrepreneurs to stay up-to-date with the latest trends and innovations. In this chapter, we will explore strategies for staying informed, identifying relevant trends, and leveraging innovations in the e-commerce industry.

38.1 Industry Research and News:

a) Subscribe to E-Commerce Publications and Newsletters:

Stay connected to the e-commerce industry by subscribing to reputable publications, newsletters, and blogs. These sources often provide insights into emerging trends, industry news, and best practices. Regularly read and analyze these resources to stay informed about the latest developments.

b) Follow Industry Influencers and Thought Leaders:

Identify influential figures and thought leaders in the e-commerce space. Follow them on social media, subscribe to their blogs, and engage with their content. These individuals often share valuable insights, trends, and predictions that can help you stay ahead of the curve.

c) Attend E-Commerce Conferences and Webinars:

Participate in e-commerce conferences, trade shows, and webinars. These events bring together industry experts, innovators, and entrepreneurs who share their knowledge and experiences. Engage in networking opportunities, attend keynote speeches, and participate in panel discussions to gain valuable insights and learn about emerging trends.

38.2 Monitoring Consumer Behavior:

a) Analyze Customer Data and Analytics:

Leverage data analytics tools to gather insights about your customers' behavior, preferences, and purchasing patterns. Analyze the data to identify emerging trends, spot changes in consumer behavior, and make data-driven decisions to optimize your e-commerce strategies.

b) Conduct Surveys and Feedback Collection:

Regularly solicit feedback from your customers through surveys, reviews, or social media polls. Ask about their preferences, shopping habits, and expectations. This direct feedback can provide valuable insights into emerging trends and help you tailor your offerings to meet customer demands.

c) Monitor Social Media and Online Communities:

Stay active on social media platforms and participate in relevant online communities and forums. Observe conversations, trends, and discussions related to e-commerce. Engage with your target audience, join relevant groups, and pay attention to their interests, pain points, and emerging demands.

38.3 Embracing Technological Innovations:

a) Keep Up with E-Commerce Technology Providers:

Stay informed about the latest updates, features, and innovations from e-commerce technology providers such as Shopify, WooCommerce, and Magento. Follow their blogs, attend webinars, and explore new tools and integrations that can enhance your e-commerce operations.

b) Embrace Mobile Commerce and Responsive Design:

With the growing prevalence of mobile devices, prioritize mobile commerce and ensure your website is optimized for mobile users. Stay updated on mobile commerce trends, such as mobile payment options and mobile-friendly user experiences, to provide a seamless shopping experience to your customers.

c) Explore Emerging Technologies:

Stay abreast of emerging technologies that have the potential to disrupt the e-commerce industry. Keep an eye on developments in areas such as artificial intelligence, virtual reality, voice commerce, and chatbots. Evaluate how these technologies can enhance your e-commerce business and improve customer experiences.

38.4 Competitive Analysis:

a) Monitor Competitors' Websites and Social Media:

Regularly visit your competitors' websites and social media profiles to analyze their strategies, offerings, and promotions. Pay attention to their customer engagement tactics, product launches, and innovations. This analysis can provide valuable insights into emerging trends and help you identify areas for improvement.

b) Benchmark Against Industry Leaders:

Study successful e-commerce companies that are considered industry leaders. Analyze their strategies, customer experiences, and innovations. Benchmark against their practices and adapt relevant strategies to suit your business goals and target market.

c) Collaborate and Network with Peers:

Engage with fellow e-commerce entrepreneurs, join industry-specific groups, and attend networking events. Collaborate and share insights with like-minded individuals to gain diverse perspectives on trends and innovations. Collaborative learning can help you uncover new opportunities and stay informed about emerging trends.

Conclusion:

Staying up-to-date with the latest trends and innovations in e-commerce is essential for long-term success. By actively researching industry news, monitoring consumer behavior, embracing technological advancements, and analyzing competitors, you can position your e-commerce business at the forefront of the industry. Continuously adapt and evolve your strategies based on the insights you gain to maintain a competitive edge.

Chapter 39: Building a Personal Brand and Establishing Yourself as a Thought Leader in Your Industry

In the competitive world of e-commerce, building a strong personal brand and establishing yourself as a thought leader can significantly differentiate you from the competition and attract loyal customers. In this chapter, we will explore strategies for building a personal brand, positioning yourself as a trusted authority, and becoming a thought leader in your industry.

39.1 Defining Your Personal Brand:

a) Identify Your Unique Value Proposition:

Determine what sets you apart from others in your industry. Identify your strengths, expertise, and passions. Craft a unique value proposition that showcases your distinct qualities and what you can offer to your target audience.

b) Define Your Brand Personality and Voice:

Develop a clear brand personality that aligns with your values and resonates with your target audience. Define your brand's voice, whether it's authoritative, friendly, or innovative. Consistently communicate in a tone that reflects your brand persona across all your online and offline interactions.

c) Create a Compelling Brand Story:

Craft a compelling brand story that highlights your journey, experiences, and motivations. Share your story through your website, social media platforms, and content to create an emotional connection with your audience. Use storytelling to engage and inspire your audience, making them feel connected to your brand.

39.2 Building Your Online Presence:

a) Develop a Professional Website or Blog:

Create a professional website or blog where you can showcase your expertise, share valuable content, and engage with your audience. Optimize your website for search engines, ensuring it reflects your personal brand and offers a seamless user experience.

b) Engage on Social Media Platforms:

Choose social media platforms that align with your target audience's preferences and actively engage with your followers. Share insightful content, respond to comments, and participate in industry conversations. Position yourself as a helpful resource and foster meaningful connections with your audience.

c) Publish Thought Leadership Content:

Consistently create and publish high-quality content that showcases your expertise and provides value to your audience. This can include blog articles, whitepapers, videos, podcasts, or social media posts. Demonstrate your industry knowledge, share insights, and offer practical advice to establish yourself as a trusted authority.

39.3 Establishing Thought Leadership:

a) Speak at Industry Events and Webinars:

Leverage speaking opportunities at industry events, conferences, and webinars to share your expertise and insights. Offer to contribute as a guest speaker or panelist, focusing on topics relevant to your niche. By sharing your knowledge with a broader audience, you can enhance your credibility and visibility.

b) Publish a Book or E-Book:

Consider writing and publishing a book or e-book within your area of expertise. This not only establishes your authority but also provides a tangible resource for your audience. Share excerpts from your book, conduct book signings, and leverage it as a marketing tool for your personal brand.

c) Collaborate with Influencers and Industry Experts:

Forge relationships with influencers and industry experts who share similar interests or target audiences. Collaborate on joint projects, guest blog on each other's platforms, or co-create content. This collaboration can help expand your reach and credibility within your industry.

39.4 Networking and Mentoring:

a) Attend Industry Events and Networking Functions:

Regularly attend industry events, trade shows, and networking functions to meet fellow professionals and potential partners. Engage in conversations, share insights, and establish meaningful connections. Networking can lead to valuable collaborations and opportunities for growth.

b) Mentor Others in Your Industry:

Share your knowledge and experience by mentoring aspiring entrepreneurs or industry newcomers. Offer guidance, support, and advice to help them navigate the e-commerce landscape. Mentoring not only establishes you as a thought leader but also allows you to give back to the community.

c) Engage in Professional Associations and Groups:

Join professional associations, online forums, and LinkedIn groups related to your industry. Actively participate in discussions, share your expertise, and contribute valuable insights. By engaging with professionals in your field, you can expand your network and establish yourself as a respected thought leader.

Conclusion:

Building a personal brand and establishing yourself as a thought leader requires consistency, authenticity, and a genuine commitment to providing value to your audience. By defining your personal brand, leveraging online platforms, publishing thought leadership content, and engaging in networking and mentoring, you can position yourself as an industry authority and attract a loyal following.

Chapter 40: Creating Passive Income Streams with Your Shopify Business

As an e-commerce entrepreneur, one of your goals may be to create passive income streams that generate revenue even when you're not actively working. In this chapter, we will explore various strategies to create passive income with your Shopify business, allowing you to earn money while you focus on other aspects of your life or pursue new ventures.

40.1 Affiliate Marketing:

a) Identify Relevant Affiliate Programs:

Research and identify affiliate programs that align with your niche and target audience. Look for products or services that complement your offerings and have affiliate programs in place. Join reputable affiliate networks or reach out directly to potential partners.

b) Promote Affiliate Products on Your Website:

Integrate affiliate marketing into your Shopify store by promoting affiliate products through blog posts, product recommendations, or dedicated affiliate pages. Write honest and helpful reviews, create engaging content, and include affiliate links. When a customer makes a purchase through your referral link, you earn a commission.

c) Optimize Affiliate Marketing Performance:

Monitor the performance of your affiliate marketing efforts. Track clicks, conversions, and revenue generated from your affiliate links. Continuously optimize your strategies, experiment with different placements and promotions, and focus on promoting high-converting affiliate products.

40.2 Print-on-Demand Products:

a) Create Custom Designs:

Leverage print-on-demand services to create unique designs for various products, such as t-shirts, hoodies, mugs, or phone cases. Use design tools or collaborate with freelance designers to create appealing and marketable designs that resonate with your target audience.

b) Set Up Print-on-Demand Integration:

Integrate print-on-demand services with your Shopify store using apps or platforms that provide seamless integration. Set up product listings, select the available products for customization, and configure pricing and fulfillment options.

c) Promote and Sell Customized Products:

Market your print-on-demand products through your Shopify store and other marketing channels. Use social media, content marketing, and influencer partnerships to showcase your designs and encourage sales. As orders come in, the print-on-demand service handles the production, packaging, and shipping, allowing you to earn passive income.

40.3 Digital Products and Downloads:

a) Identify Marketable Digital Products:

Create digital products that provide value to your target audience. This can include e-books, online courses, templates, software, or photography presets. Identify areas where your expertise aligns with customer demands and develop products accordingly.

b) Set Up Digital Product Delivery:

Use Shopify's digital product delivery features or third-party apps to securely deliver your digital products to customers. Ensure a smooth and automated process for purchasing, downloading, and accessing the digital products.

c) Market and Sell Digital Products:

Market your digital products through your website, email marketing, content marketing, and social media. Highlight the benefits and features of your digital products, and offer special promotions or bundles to drive sales. Once set up, the sales of digital products can generate passive income with minimal ongoing effort.

40.4 Dropshipping Expansion:

a) Identify Additional Product Categories:

Expand your dropshipping business by identifying new product categories that align with your niche and target audience. Research market demand, identify reliable suppliers, and add new products to your store.

b) Optimize Product Listings and SEO:

Optimize the SEO elements of your new product listings to attract organic traffic from search engines. Use relevant keywords, create compelling product descriptions, and optimize your product images and titles. Improve your store's visibility to generate consistent sales.

c) Automate Order Fulfillment:

Utilize automation tools and systems to streamline order fulfillment processes. Set up automatic order notifications, shipment tracking, and customer support systems to minimize manual tasks and save time.

Conclusion:

Creating passive income streams with your Shopify business allows you to generate revenue without actively trading your time for money. By exploring strategies such as affiliate marketing, print-on-demand products, digital downloads, and expanding your dropshipping business, you can build additional income streams that work for you even when you're not actively involved. Continuously monitor and optimize these passive income streams to maximize their potential.

Chapter 41: Managing Your Time Effectively and Balancing Work and Life

As an e-commerce entrepreneur, managing your time effectively and finding a balance between work and personal life is crucial for your overall well-being and success. In this chapter, we will explore strategies and techniques to help you optimize your time management skills, maintain productivity, and achieve a healthy work-life balance.

41.1 Prioritizing Your Tasks and Setting Goals:

a) Identify Your Most Important Tasks:

Start your day by identifying the most important tasks that align with your business goals. Prioritize tasks based on their urgency, importance, and impact on your business. Focus on completing these tasks first before moving on to less critical ones.

b) Set SMART Goals:

Establish specific, measurable, achievable, relevant, and time-bound (SMART) goals for both your short-term and long-term objectives. Break down these goals into actionable steps, and create a timeline to track your progress. Having clear goals helps you stay focused and motivated.

d) Use Task Management Tools:

Utilize task management tools or project management software to keep track of your tasks, deadlines, and progress. These tools help you stay organized, delegate tasks, and collaborate with team members efficiently. Find a system that works for you and allows you to stay on top of your responsibilities.

41.2 Time Blocking and Effective Scheduling:

a) Time Blocking Method:

Implement the time blocking method to allocate specific time blocks for different tasks or activities. Set aside dedicated blocks for focused work, meetings, email management, and personal activities. This technique helps you structure your day, manage interruptions, and improve productivity.

b) Create a Daily Schedule:

Create a daily schedule that includes your work-related tasks, breaks, and personal activities. Set realistic time frames for each task and be mindful of your energy levels throughout the day. Be disciplined in following your schedule while allowing flexibility for unforeseen circumstances.

c) Batch Similar Tasks:

Group similar tasks together and complete them in batches. For example, dedicate a specific time block for responding to emails, another for content creation, and another for customer support. Batching tasks improves efficiency by minimizing context switching and maximizing focus.

41.3 Effective Delegation and Outsourcing:

a) Identify Tasks to Delegate:

Identify tasks that can be delegated to others, whether it's hiring employees, freelancers, or outsourcing certain aspects of your business. Delegate tasks that are time-consuming, repetitive, or outside your area of expertise. This frees up your time to focus on higher-value activities.

b) Build a Reliable Team:

Invest time in building a reliable and competent team. Hire employees or contractors who have the skills and expertise to handle delegated tasks effectively. Provide clear instructions, set expectations, and establish channels of communication to ensure smooth collaboration.

c) Leverage Automation and Tools:

Take advantage of automation tools and software to streamline repetitive tasks. Automate email marketing, social media scheduling, order fulfillment, and customer support processes. Identify areas where technology can help you save time and optimize efficiency.

41.4 Setting Boundaries and Practicing Self-Care:

a) Establish Work-Life Boundaries:

Define clear boundaries between work and personal life. Set specific working hours and communicate them to your team, clients, and stakeholders. Avoid checking work-related emails or engaging in work tasks outside of these designated hours.

b) Take Regular Breaks:

Schedule regular breaks throughout your workday to rest, recharge, and avoid burnout. Step away from your workspace, engage in physical activity, practice mindfulness, or pursue hobbies that bring you joy. Taking breaks enhances productivity and mental well-being.

c) Practice Self-Care:

Prioritize self-care activities such as exercise, proper nutrition, and sufficient sleep. Nurture your physical and mental health to sustain high productivity levels and prevent exhaustion. Establish self-care routines and rituals that support your overall well-being.

Conclusion:

Effective time management and maintaining a healthy work-life balance are essential for your long-term success as an e-commerce entrepreneur. By prioritizing tasks, implementing time blocking, delegating effectively, and setting boundaries, you can optimize your productivity and achieve harmony between work and personal life. Remember to practice self-care and make time for activities that bring you joy and fulfillment.

Chapter 42: Maintaining a Healthy Work/Life Balance as Your Business Grows

As your e-commerce business grows, it's important to continuously prioritize maintaining a healthy work-life balance. Scaling your business can often lead to increased responsibilities and demands on your time. In this chapter, we will explore strategies to help you effectively manage your workload, delegate tasks, and find harmony between your professional and personal life.

42.1 Assessing Your Workload and Priorities:

a) Regularly Review Your Tasks and Responsibilities:

As your business grows, regularly assess your workload and responsibilities. Identify tasks that can be streamlined, automated, or delegated to free up your time for higher-value activities. Prioritize tasks that align with your core competencies and contribute to your business's growth.

b) Set Realistic Expectations and Boundaries:

Be realistic about what you can accomplish within a given timeframe. Avoid overcommitting or taking on excessive responsibilities that may compromise your work-life balance. Set clear boundaries with clients, employees, and partners to manage expectations and create a sustainable workload.

c) Focus on High-Impact Activities:

Identify high-impact activities that drive significant results for your business. Prioritize tasks that directly contribute to revenue generation, strategic planning, and business growth. Delegate or outsource tasks that are time-consuming but do not require your direct involvement.

42.2 Effective Delegation and Empowering Your Team:

a) Delegate with Clarity:

Develop a clear delegation process and communicate expectations and responsibilities to your team members. Clearly define tasks, provide necessary resources and guidance, and establish checkpoints for progress updates. Trust your team to handle delegated tasks competently.

b) Empower Your Team:

Invest in training and development for your team members to enhance their skills and capabilities. Encourage autonomy and decision-making within their areas of responsibility. Empowering your team not only lightens your workload but also fosters a sense of ownership and commitment.

c) Regularly Communicate and Provide Feedback:

Maintain open lines of communication with your team members. Schedule regular check-ins, team meetings, or one-on-one discussions to provide feedback, address challenges, and ensure alignment with your business objectives. Effective communication strengthens collaboration and helps maintain accountability.

42.3 Time Management and Prioritization Techniques:

a) Time Blocking and Calendar Management:

Continue to use time blocking techniques to structure your schedule effectively. Prioritize tasks, allocate specific time blocks for different activities, and guard those time slots against interruptions. Utilize calendar management tools to plan and visualize your commitments.

b) Practice the Pomodoro Technique:

Implement the Pomodoro Technique, a time management method that involves working in focused intervals, typically 25 minutes, followed by short breaks. This technique helps maintain focus and productivity while incorporating regular breaks to prevent burnout.

c) Leverage Productivity Tools:

Explore productivity tools and apps that can help you streamline your workflow, manage tasks, and improve efficiency. Use project management software, task trackers, and time management apps to stay organized and optimize your productivity.

42.4 Self-Care and Well-Being:

a) Set Aside Personal Time:

Schedule personal time for self-care, hobbies, family, and friends. Dedicate specific time slots each day or week for activities that bring you joy and relaxation. Protect this time as non-negotiable and prioritize your well-being.

b) Practice Mindfulness and Stress Management:

Incorporate mindfulness and stress management techniques into your routine. Engage in activities such as meditation, yoga, or deep breathing exercises to reduce stress and maintain mental clarity. Take breaks throughout the day to rejuvenate your mind and prevent burnout.

c) Foster Work-Life Integration:

Seek opportunities to integrate work and personal life where possible. For example, consider flexible work arrangements that allow you to attend personal events or pursue personal interests during non-traditional work hours. Strive for a harmonious blend of work and personal life that supports your overall well-being.

Conclusion:

As your e-commerce business grows, maintaining a healthy work-life balance becomes even more critical. By assessing your workload, effectively delegating tasks, managing your time, and prioritizing self-care, you can find harmony between your professional and personal life. Remember that maintaining balance is an ongoing process that requires regular evaluation and adjustments. By implementing these strategies, you can ensure your own well-being while driving the continued success of your business.

Chapter 43: Overcoming Challenges and Setbacks as an Entrepreneur

Being an entrepreneur is not without its challenges and setbacks. In this chapter, we will explore strategies to help you navigate through tough times, overcome obstacles, and bounce back stronger. By adopting a resilient mindset and implementing effective problem-solving techniques, you can turn challenges into opportunities for growth and success.

43.1 Embracing a Resilient Mindset:

a) Accepting the Reality of Challenges:

Recognize that challenges and setbacks are a natural part of the entrepreneurial journey. Accepting this reality allows you to approach difficulties with a proactive and solutions-oriented mindset.

b) Cultivating a Growth Mindset:

Develop a growth mindset that sees challenges as opportunities for learning and personal development. Embrace the belief that you can learn from setbacks, adapt, and improve your strategies moving forward.

c) Seeking Support and Perspective:

Reach out to mentors, fellow entrepreneurs, or support networks to gain insights and perspectives from others who have faced similar challenges. Surround yourself with a positive and supportive community that can offer guidance and encouragement.

43.2 Effective Problem-Solving Techniques:

a) Identify the Root Cause:

When faced with a challenge, dig deep to identify the root cause of the problem. Ask critical questions to uncover underlying issues that may have contributed to the setback. Understanding the root cause allows you to develop targeted solutions.

b) Break the Problem into Smaller Steps:

Break down the challenge into smaller, more manageable tasks. This approach helps prevent overwhelm and allows you to tackle the problem step by step. Focus on making progress in incremental stages.

c) Brainstorm Solutions:

Engage in brainstorming sessions to generate potential solutions. Encourage creative thinking and explore different perspectives. Consider involving your team or seeking input from trusted advisors to gain diverse insights.

d) Test and Iterate:

Implement a test-and-iterate approach to problem-solving. Pilot new strategies or solutions on a smaller scale before implementing them fully. Collect feedback, analyze results, and refine your approach based on real-world data.

43.3 Resilience in the Face of Setbacks:

a) Learn from Failures:

View failures as valuable learning experiences. Analyze what went wrong, identify lessons learned, and adjust your strategies accordingly. Embrace failure as an opportunity for growth and improvement.

b) Maintain a Positive Mindset:

Even in challenging times, maintain a positive mindset. Focus on the lessons learned, the progress made, and the opportunities that lie ahead. Surround yourself with positive influences and practice gratitude for what you have accomplished.

c) Seek Solutions, Not Blame:

When setbacks occur, resist the temptation to blame others or dwell on negativity. Instead, focus on finding solutions and taking ownership of the situation. Look for opportunities to collaborate, seek expert advice, or pivot your approach.

43.4 Persistence and Adaptability:

a) Stay Committed to Your Vision:

Remind yourself of your long-term vision and goals. Maintain unwavering commitment to your entrepreneurial journey, even in the face of challenges. Use setbacks as motivation to persevere and keep moving forward.

b) Embrace Flexibility and Adaptation:

Entrepreneurship requires adaptability. Be willing to pivot your strategies, adjust your plans, and embrace change when necessary. Stay agile and open to new opportunities that may arise from setbacks.

c) Celebrate Small Victories:

Acknowledge and celebrate small victories along the way. Recognize that progress is not always linear, and even small steps forward contribute to your overall success. Cultivate a positive and optimistic mindset that acknowledges and appreciates progress, no matter how small.

Conclusion:

As an entrepreneur, challenges and setbacks are inevitable, but with the right mindset and problem-solving techniques, you can overcome them and continue on your path to success. Embrace a resilient mindset, seek support when needed, and approach challenges with a proactive attitude. Remember that setbacks can be valuable opportunities for growth and innovation. By persisting, adapting, and maintaining a positive outlook, you will be better equipped to navigate the entrepreneurial journey.

Chapter 44: Staying Motivated and Focused on Your Goals

As an entrepreneur, staying motivated and focused on your goals is crucial for long-term success. In this chapter, we will explore strategies to help you maintain your motivation, overcome obstacles, and stay laser-focused on achieving your entrepreneurial aspirations.

44.1 Clarifying Your Goals and Vision:

a) Define Your Long-Term Vision:

Take the time to clearly define your long-term vision for your business. Visualize where you want to be in the future and set ambitious but achievable goals that align with your vision.

b) Break Down Your Goals into Milestones:

Break down your long-term goals into smaller, actionable milestones. This allows you to track progress and celebrate achievements along the way. Each milestone brings you closer to your ultimate vision, keeping you motivated and focused.

c) Establish Clear and Measurable Objectives:

Set clear and measurable objectives for each milestone. This enables you to track your progress and stay accountable to yourself and your team. Clear objectives provide a sense of direction and purpose, helping you maintain focus.

44.2 Cultivating Motivation:

a) Find Your "Why":

Identify your deeper reasons and motivations behind your entrepreneurial journey. Understand the impact you want to make, the values you hold dear, and the personal fulfillment you seek. Connect with your "why" to fuel your motivation.

b) Surround Yourself with Inspiration:

Surround yourself with positive influences and seek inspiration from others who have achieved similar goals. Engage in networking events, attend conferences, read books, or listen to podcasts that feature successful entrepreneurs. These interactions can reignite your motivation and provide valuable insights.

c) Celebrate Small Wins:

Acknowledge and celebrate your achievements, no matter how small they may seem. Recognize that progress is made one step at a time, and each accomplishment brings you closer to your goals. Celebrating small wins boosts motivation and keeps you on track.

d) Create a Supportive Environment:

Surround yourself with a supportive network of like-minded individuals who understand and encourage your entrepreneurial journey. Seek out mentors, join mastermind groups, or engage in online communities where you can share experiences, gain insights, and find support.

44.3 Overcoming Challenges:

a) Embrace a Growth Mindset:

View challenges as opportunities for growth and learning. Cultivate a mindset that sees setbacks as stepping stones toward success. Embrace challenges as chances to innovate, improve, and develop resilience.

b) Break Down Complex Problems:

When faced with complex challenges, break them down into smaller, manageable parts. This approach allows you to tackle each component individually, reducing overwhelm and making problem-solving more attainable.

c) Seek Support and Guidance:

Don't hesitate to seek support and guidance when facing challenges. Reach out to mentors, advisors, or peers who can offer fresh perspectives and potential solutions. Collaboration and input from others can help you overcome obstacles more effectively.

d) Learn from Setbacks:

When setbacks occur, take the opportunity to learn and grow. Reflect on the lessons gained from each setback and adjust your strategies accordingly. Use setbacks as stepping stones to become a stronger and more resilient entrepreneur.

44.4 Maintaining Focus:

a) Prioritize Your Tasks:

Focus on the most important tasks that align with your goals and have the highest impact on your business. Use prioritization techniques like the Eisenhower Matrix or the 80/20 rule to allocate your time and energy effectively.

b) Minimize Distractions:

Identify and minimize distractions that can derail your focus. Set boundaries with technology, establish a designated workspace, and manage interruptions to create an environment conducive to concentration and productivity.

c) Practice Time Management:

Implement effective time management techniques to optimize your productivity. Break your work into manageable chunks, utilize productivity tools and apps, and establish routines that promote focused work periods.

d) Regularly Review and Adjust:

Regularly review your goals, milestones, and progress. Assess what is working and what needs adjustment. By periodically reevaluating your focus and making necessary adjustments, you ensure that your efforts remain aligned with your evolving vision.

Conclusion:

Staying motivated and focused on your goals is essential for the success of your entrepreneurial journey. Clarify your long-term vision, cultivate motivation through your "why," and create a supportive environment that keeps you inspired. Overcome challenges with a growth mindset, break down complex problems, and seek support when needed. Maintain focus by prioritizing tasks, minimizing distractions, and practicing effective time management. By applying these strategies, you will stay on track, achieve your goals, and realize your entrepreneurial dreams.

Chapter 45: Avoiding Common Mistakes and Pitfalls of E-Commerce Businesses

Running an e-commerce business can be a rewarding and profitable venture, but it's not without its challenges. In this chapter, we will discuss common mistakes and pitfalls that e-commerce entrepreneurs often encounter, and provide strategies to help you avoid them. By learning from the experiences of others, you can navigate the e-commerce landscape more effectively and increase your chances of success.

45.1 Insufficient Market Research:

a) Understanding Customer Needs:

Conduct thorough market research to gain a deep understanding of your target audience's needs, preferences, and pain points. By knowing your customers well, you can tailor your products, marketing, and customer experience to meet their expectations.

b) Assessing Market Demand:

Evaluate the market demand for your products or services before launching your e-commerce business. Identify potential competitors, analyze market trends, and assess the viability of your business idea. This research will help you determine if there is sufficient demand for your offerings.

c) Testing the Market:

Consider conducting market tests or soft launches to gauge customer interest and gather feedback before fully investing in your e-commerce business. This approach allows you to validate your business idea and make adjustments based on early customer responses.

45.2 Poor Website Design and User Experience:

a) Responsive and Mobile-Friendly Design:

Ensure that your e-commerce website is optimized for mobile devices. A responsive design that provides a seamless user experience across different screen sizes and devices is crucial for capturing and retaining customers.

b) Clear and Intuitive Navigation:

Simplify the navigation structure of your website to make it easy for visitors to find products, browse categories, and complete purchases. Use clear and concise labeling, intuitive menus, and search functionality to enhance the user experience.

c) Fast Loading Speed:

Optimize the loading speed of your website to prevent potential customers from abandoning your site due to slow performance. Compress images, leverage caching techniques, and choose a reliable hosting provider to ensure fast and efficient website loading times.

45.3 Ineffective Marketing and Customer Acquisition:

a)Targeted Marketing Strategies:

Develop a comprehensive marketing strategy that includes a mix of tactics such as search engine optimization (SEO), content marketing, social media advertising, influencer partnerships, and email marketing. Tailor your marketing efforts to reach your target audience effectively.

b) Customer Relationship Building:

Focus on building strong relationships with your customers through personalized communication, exceptional customer service, and loyalty programs. Nurture customer loyalty to encourage repeat purchases and positive word-of-mouth referrals.

c) Analytics and Performance Tracking:

Leverage analytics tools to track the performance of your marketing campaigns and website. Monitor key metrics such as conversion rates, customer acquisition costs, and customer lifetime value to make data-driven decisions and optimize your marketing efforts.

45.4 Inadequate Inventory Management:

a) Accurate Demand Forecasting:

Implement robust inventory management systems to accurately forecast demand and avoid stockouts or overstocking. Monitor sales trends, analyze historical data, and consider seasonality or product lifecycle factors to optimize your inventory levels.

b) Efficient Supply Chain:

Establish strong relationships with reliable suppliers and streamline your supply chain processes to ensure timely and efficient product delivery. Implement inventory replenishment strategies, monitor supplier performance, and maintain clear communication channels.

c) Inventory Optimization:

Regularly assess your inventory turnover ratio and identify slow-moving or obsolete products. Optimize your product mix, liquidate excess inventory strategically, and consider implementing dropshipping or just-in-time inventory practices to reduce holding costs.

45.5 Neglecting Customer Service:

a) Prompt and Responsive Communication:

Prioritize timely and helpful communication with your customers. Respond promptly to inquiries, provide clear and accurate information, and resolve issues or complaints in a professional and satisfactory manner.

b) Proactive Order Status Updates:

Keep your customers informed about their order status, shipping updates, and any potential delays. Provide tracking information and proactive notifications to enhance transparency and build trust with your customers.

c) Post-Purchase Support and Follow-Up:

Offer post-purchase support to ensure customer satisfaction. Follow up with customers after their purchase to gather feedback, address any concerns, and provide assistance if needed. Engage with customers through email marketing or loyalty programs to foster long-term relationships.

Conclusion:

By avoiding common mistakes and pitfalls that e-commerce businesses often encounter, you can increase your chances of success. Conduct thorough market research, prioritize website design and user experience, develop effective marketing and customer acquisition strategies, implement efficient inventory management practices, and provide exceptional customer service. Learn from the experiences of other entrepreneurs and continuously adapt and improve your business. By applying these strategies, you will be better equipped to navigate the challenges of running an e-commerce business and build a thriving online venture.

Chapter 46: Building Resilience and Adaptability to Navigate Market Changes and Disruptions

In the dynamic world of e-commerce, market changes and disruptions are inevitable. To thrive in such an environment, e-commerce entrepreneurs need to develop resilience and adaptability. In this chapter, we will explore strategies to build resilience, embrace change, and adapt your business to navigate market shifts successfully.

46.1 Developing a Growth Mindset:

a) Embrace Change:

Adopt a growth mindset that sees challenges as opportunities for growth. Instead of fearing or resisting change, embrace it as a chance to learn, innovate, and adapt your business to evolving market conditions.

b) Cultivate a Learning Attitude:

Continuously seek knowledge and stay updated with industry trends. Invest in your own personal and professional development through courses, workshops, and networking events. Encourage your team members to engage in continuous learning as well.

c) Foster a Culture of Innovation:

Create an environment where creativity and innovation are valued. Encourage your team to generate new ideas, experiment with different approaches, and embrace calculated risks. Celebrate both successes and failures as opportunities for learning and improvement.

46.2 Building a Flexible Business Model:

a) Diversify Your Product Range:

Offer a diverse range of products or services to cater to different customer segments and mitigate the risk of relying too heavily on a single product or niche. Continuously assess market demand and expand your product offerings strategically.

b) Explore New Sales Channels:

Consider expanding your presence beyond your Shopify store. Explore opportunities to sell on other e-commerce platforms, marketplaces, or through brick-and-mortar partnerships. Diversifying your sales channels can help you reach a wider audience and reduce reliance on a single platform.

c) Adapt Pricing and Promotions:

Monitor market trends and adjust your pricing and promotional strategies accordingly. Be flexible with your pricing to remain competitive while maintaining profitability. Experiment with different promotional tactics to attract and retain customers.

46.3 Nurturing Customer Relationships:

a) Listen to Customer Feedback:

Actively seek feedback from your customers through surveys, reviews, and social media interactions. Use this feedback to identify areas for improvement and adjust your products, services, or customer experience accordingly.

b) Anticipate Customer Needs:

Stay attuned to evolving customer preferences and anticipate their changing needs. Regularly analyze customer data, monitor industry trends, and engage in market research to identify emerging opportunities and adjust your business strategy accordingly.

c) Provide Exceptional Customer Service:

Invest in building a customer-centric culture within your organization. Train your customer service team to deliver exceptional support, handle customer inquiries promptly, and resolve issues effectively. A strong reputation for excellent customer service can help you navigate market changes more smoothly.

46.4 Building Strong Supplier Relationships:

a) Maintain Open Communication:

Develop strong and transparent relationships with your suppliers. Maintain open lines of communication to stay informed about any potential disruptions or changes in the supply chain. Regularly assess supplier performance and address any issues proactively.

b) Diversify Your Supplier Network:

Avoid relying too heavily on a single supplier. Diversify your supplier network to mitigate the risk of disruptions or shortages. Cultivate relationships with multiple suppliers who can provide similar products or materials.

c) Continuously Evaluate and Optimize:

Regularly evaluate your supplier relationships based on factors such as quality, reliability, pricing, and responsiveness. Continuously seek opportunities to optimize your supply chain and improve efficiency.

Conclusion:

Building resilience and adaptability is essential for navigating market changes and disruptions in the e-commerce industry. Develop a growth mindset, embrace change, and foster a culture of innovation within your organization. Build a flexible business model that allows you to diversify your product range and explore new sales channels. Nurturing customer relationships and maintaining strong supplier connections are also key. By implementing these strategies, you will be better prepared to navigate market shifts, seize new opportunities, and build a thriving e-commerce business.

Chapter 47: Preparing for Exit Strategies and Selling Your Shopify Business

As an e-commerce entrepreneur, it's essential to plan for the future, including the possibility of selling your Shopify business. Whether you're considering an exit strategy in the near term or simply want to be prepared for the future, this chapter will guide you through the process of preparing for a successful sale of your e-commerce business.

47.1 Assessing the Right Time to Sell:

a) Business Performance:

Evaluate your business's financial performance, growth trajectory, and overall profitability. Consider selling during a period of strong performance, as this can increase the value and attractiveness of your business to potential buyers.

b) Market Conditions:

Monitor market conditions and industry trends to determine the optimal timing for a sale. If the e-commerce market is experiencing significant growth and there is high demand for businesses in your niche, it may be an opportune time to sell.

c) Personal Factors:

Consider personal circumstances, such as changes in your goals, interests, or life situation, that may influence your decision to sell. Assess whether you have the time, resources, and motivation to continue growing the business or if it's the right time to pursue other ventures.

47.2 Maximizing the Value of Your Business:

a) Financial Documentation:

Ensure your financial records are accurate, up to date, and well-documented. This includes financial statements, tax filings, sales records, and other relevant financial information. Organized and transparent financial documentation can instill confidence in potential buyers.

b) Intellectual Property and Legal Matters:

Protect your intellectual property rights, including trademarks, patents, or copyrights associated with your brand. Resolve any legal issues, such as pending lawsuits or disputes, to mitigate risks for potential buyers.

c) Diversified Customer Base:

Demonstrate that your business has a diverse and loyal customer base. Reduce reliance on a single customer or a few major accounts to make your business more attractive to potential buyers. Showcase customer retention rates, repeat purchase patterns, and positive customer reviews.

d) Growth Opportunities:

Highlight potential growth opportunities for the business. Showcase untapped markets, product expansion possibilities, or new revenue streams that can be pursued by the buyer. Providing a clear growth strategy can increase the perceived value of your business.

47.3 Finding the Right Buyer:

a) Confidentiality:

Maintain confidentiality throughout the selling process to protect the sensitive information and reputation of your business. Use non-disclosure agreements (NDAs) when sharing confidential information with potential buyers or engage the services of a trusted business broker.

b) Networking and Connections:

Leverage your industry connections and network to find potential buyers. Attend industry events, join e-commerce forums, or engage with other entrepreneurs to identify potential buyers who may be interested in acquiring a business like yours.

c) Engaging Professionals:

Consider working with professionals such as business brokers, accountants, or lawyers experienced in e-commerce business sales. They can help you navigate the complexities of the selling process, identify qualified buyers, and negotiate favorable terms.

47.4 Negotiating the Sale:

a) Valuation and Pricing:

Determine a realistic and competitive asking price for your business. Consider factors such as financial performance, growth potential, market conditions, and industry benchmarks. Be prepared to negotiate with potential buyers to reach a mutually beneficial agreement.

b) Due Diligence:

Be prepared to provide detailed information and documentation to potential buyers during the due diligence process. This includes financial records, operational data, customer insights, and legal documentation. Respond promptly to buyer inquiries and address any concerns transparently.

c) Structuring the Deal:

Work with professionals to structure the deal in a way that aligns with your goals and minimizes risks. Consider options such as an outright sale, partial sale, or earn-out arrangement. Carefully review and negotiate the terms of the purchase agreement, including payment terms and any post-sale obligations.

Conclusion:

Preparing for the sale of your Shopify business requires careful planning, attention to detail, and strategic decision-making. Assess the right time to sell, maximize the value of your business, find the right buyer, and negotiate the sale terms. Engage professionals to guide you through the process and ensure a smooth transition. By following these steps, you can increase the likelihood of a successful sale and achieve your desired outcome.

Chapter 48: Creating a Legacy of Success and Impact through Your Business

Beyond financial success, many entrepreneurs aspire to create a lasting impact and leave a meaningful legacy through their business. In this chapter, we will explore strategies for building a business that goes beyond profitability and makes a positive difference in the world. We will discuss how you can align your business with your values, contribute to social and environmental causes, and inspire others to follow your example.

48.1 Defining Your Business Values and Purpose:

a) Reflecting on Your Values:

Take time to reflect on your personal values and how they align with your business goals. Identify the values that drive you, such as integrity, sustainability, social responsibility, or innovation.

b) Defining Your Business Purpose:

Clarify the purpose of your business beyond financial success. Ask yourself how your products or services can create value for customers and positively impact the world. Define a mission statement that encapsulates your business purpose.

c) Communicating Your Values and Purpose:

Ensure that your values and purpose are clearly communicated to your team, customers, and stakeholders. Integrate them into your branding, marketing materials, and company culture to create a sense of shared purpose and attract like-minded individuals.

48.2 Integrating Social and Environmental Responsibility:

a) Ethical Sourcing and Supply Chain:

Evaluate your supply chain and consider partnering with suppliers who adhere to ethical practices. Ensure that your products are sourced responsibly, minimizing environmental impact and respecting human rights.

b) Sustainable Operations:

Adopt sustainable practices within your business operations. Reduce waste, conserve energy, and explore environmentally friendly packaging options. Incorporate sustainability into your decision-making processes and seek innovative ways to lessen your ecological footprint.

c) Corporate Social Responsibility:

Engage in initiatives that benefit your community and society at large. Support local causes, donate a portion of your profits to charitable organizations, or initiate programs that address social issues. Encourage your team members to volunteer and get involved in community service.

48.3 Inspiring and Empowering Others:

a) Employee Engagement:

Create a work environment that fosters employee growth, well-being, and fulfillment. Provide opportunities for professional development, prioritize work-life balance, and recognize and reward employees for their contributions. Empowered and engaged employees can become ambassadors for your business values and mission.

b) Collaboration and Partnerships:

Collaborate with other businesses, organizations, or entrepreneurs who share your values. Seek opportunities to work together on projects or initiatives that align with your purpose. Joint efforts can amplify your impact and inspire a broader community.

c) Sharing Your Journey:

Document and share your business journey, including the challenges, successes, and lessons learned. Share stories and experiences that reflect your values and purpose. Inspire others by demonstrating that it's possible to build a successful business while making a positive impact.

48.4 Measuring and Communicating Impact:

a) Impact Measurement:

Develop metrics and methods to measure the impact of your business. Track key performance indicators (KPIs) that reflect your social and environmental goals. This will help you assess the effectiveness of your efforts and make data-driven decisions.

b) Transparent Reporting:

Communicate your impact transparently to stakeholders. Share progress reports, social responsibility initiatives, and sustainability achievements through your website, social media platforms, and annual reports. This builds trust and demonstrates your commitment to creating a lasting impact.

c) Engaging Customers:

Involve your customers in your impact initiatives. Educate them about the social and environmental aspects of your business and invite their feedback and ideas. Encourage them to join you on your mission and make informed choices that align with their values.

Conclusion:

Creating a legacy of success and impact through your business requires a deliberate and purposeful approach. Define your values and purpose, integrate social and environmental responsibility, inspire and empower others, and measure and communicate your impact. By aligning your business with your values and making a positive difference, you can leave a lasting legacy that extends beyond financial success.

Chapter 49: Giving Back and Supporting Social Causes through Your Business

As a Shopify entrepreneur, you have the opportunity to use your business as a force for good by giving back and supporting social causes. In this chapter, we will explore different ways you can contribute to society, make a positive impact, and create a business that goes beyond profit. We will discuss strategies for incorporating philanthropy and social responsibility into your business model, engaging your customers and community, and creating a culture of giving.

49.1 Aligning Your Business with Social Causes:

a) Identifying Relevant Causes:

Reflect on social issues that align with your business values and purpose. Consider causes such as education, environmental conservation, poverty alleviation, health, or human rights. Choose causes that resonate with your customers and stakeholders.

b) Mission-Driven Business Model:

Integrate social impact into your business model. Explore opportunities to directly contribute a portion of your sales or profits to support social causes. Consider adopting a "buy-one-give-one" model or partnering with charitable organizations to donate a percentage of each sale.

c) Ethical and Sustainable Practices:

Ensure that your business operations adhere to ethical and sustainable practices. This includes responsible sourcing, fair labor practices, and minimizing your environmental footprint. Operating your business in an ethical and sustainable manner is a form of social responsibility in itself.

49.2 Engaging Your Customers and Community:

a) Communicating Your Social Impact:

Educate your customers about the social causes you support and the impact of their purchases. Use your website, social media platforms, and packaging to share stories and updates about the positive change your business is making. Transparent communication builds trust and encourages customer engagement.

b) Collaborating with Customers:

Involve your customers in your philanthropic efforts. Offer them the opportunity to contribute directly through donations or volunteering. Consider organizing events or campaigns where customers can actively participate in supporting social causes alongside your business.

c) Community Involvement:

Engage with your local community by supporting local events, organizations, or initiatives. Sponsor or participate in community projects that address pressing social issues.

Building strong relationships with your community fosters goodwill and strengthens your business's reputation.

49.3 Creating a Culture of Giving:

a) Employee Volunteer Programs:

Encourage your employees to volunteer their time and skills for social causes. Establish a structured employee volunteer program that allows them to engage in community service during work hours. This not only supports the causes you care about but also boosts employee morale and engagement.

b) Donation Matching:

Implement a donation matching program where you match employee donations to charitable organizations. This demonstrates your commitment to giving back and encourages employees to contribute to causes they are passionate about.

c) Partnering with Nonprofits:

Form strategic partnerships with nonprofits or charitable organizations that align with your values. Collaborate on joint initiatives, campaigns, or events that amplify your impact and leverage their expertise. This partnership can provide additional resources and create meaningful change.

49.4 Measuring and Communicating Impact:

a) Impact Assessment:

Develop metrics and methods to measure the impact of your social initiatives. Track key performance indicators (KPIs) that reflect the outcomes and reach of your contributions. Regularly assess and evaluate the effectiveness of your philanthropic efforts.

b) Storytelling and Reporting:

Share success stories and impact reports that showcase the difference your business is making. Use storytelling techniques to connect emotionally with your audience and inspire them to support your cause. Communicate your impact through various channels, such as social media, newsletters, and annual reports.

c) Collaboration and Knowledge Sharing:

Collaborate with other businesses and entrepreneurs who are committed to social responsibility. Share best practices, lessons learned, and innovative ideas for creating a positive social impact. By collaborating and sharing knowledge, you can collectively drive greater change.

Conclusion:

Giving back and supporting social causes through your Shopify business is a powerful way to make a positive impact in society. Align your business with social causes, engage your customers and community, create a culture of giving within your organization, and measure and communicate your impact. By integrating philanthropy and social responsibility into your business, you can create a meaningful legacy and inspire others to contribute to positive change.

Chapter 50: Living a Fulfilling and Meaningful Life as an Entrepreneur

Being an entrepreneur is not just about building a successful business; it's also about living a fulfilling and meaningful life. In this final chapter, we will explore strategies for finding balance, maintaining well-being, and cultivating a sense of purpose as an entrepreneur. We will discuss how to prioritize self-care, nurture personal relationships, and make a positive impact beyond your business.

50.1 Prioritizing Self-Care:

a) Physical Well-being:

Take care of your physical health by incorporating regular exercise, nutritious meals, and adequate sleep into your routine. Prioritize self-care activities like yoga, meditation, or hobbies that promote relaxation and rejuvenation.

b) Mental Well-being:

Manage stress and maintain mental well-being by practicing mindfulness, setting boundaries, and engaging in activities that bring you joy and fulfillment. Take breaks, disconnect from work, and seek support from mentors, coaches, or therapists when needed.

c) Work-Life Balance:

Strive for a healthy work-life balance by setting clear boundaries between work and personal life. Allocate dedicated time for family, hobbies, and activities that bring you happiness and fulfillment. Learn to delegate and outsource tasks to create more time for yourself.

50.2 Nurturing Personal Relationships:

a) Quality Time with Loved Ones:

Make time for your loved ones and prioritize meaningful connections. Schedule regular quality time with your family and friends, create traditions, and engage in activities that strengthen your relationships. Be present and attentive during these moments.

b) Building a Support Network:

Cultivate a strong support network of like-minded entrepreneurs, mentors, and friends who understand the challenges you face. Surround yourself with individuals who inspire and motivate you. Lean on your support network for guidance, advice, and encouragement.

c) Giving Back to the Community:

Extend your impact beyond your business by engaging in philanthropic activities as a family or a team. Volunteer together, support local charities, or initiate community projects. Engaging in acts of service can bring joy, fulfillment, and a sense of purpose to your personal life.

50.3 Cultivating a Sense of Purpose:

a) Reflecting on Your Values and Passions:

Continually reflect on your values and passions to ensure that your business aligns with them. Explore opportunities to integrate your personal passions into your business activities. This alignment creates a sense of purpose and fulfillment.

b) Setting Meaningful Goals:

Set meaningful goals that go beyond financial success. Define personal and professional goals that align with your values and contribute to your sense of purpose. Regularly assess your progress and make adjustments as needed.

c) Making a Positive Impact:

Identify ways to make a positive impact in your community or the world. Use your business platform to support causes that are meaningful to you. Whether it's through charitable donations, sustainability efforts, or social initiatives, strive to leave a positive mark on the world.

50.4 Continuous Learning and Personal Growth:

a) Lifelong Learning:

Commit to lifelong learning and personal growth. Stay curious, explore new interests, and seek opportunities to expand your knowledge and skills. This not only enhances your entrepreneurial journey but also contributes to personal fulfillment.

b) Embracing Failure and Resilience:

View failures as opportunities for growth and learning. Embrace challenges and setbacks as part of the entrepreneurial journey, and develop resilience to overcome them. Learn from your experiences, adapt, and continue to grow.

c) Celebrating Achievements:

Acknowledge and celebrate your achievements along the way. Take time to reflect on your progress and milestones. Celebrating both small and significant accomplishments helps maintain motivation and a sense of fulfillment.

Conclusion:

Living a fulfilling and meaningful life as an entrepreneur goes beyond business success. Prioritize self-care, nurture personal relationships, cultivate a sense of purpose, and commit to continuous learning and personal growth. Remember that your well-being and happiness are essential for sustaining long-term success. By finding balance and purpose in your entrepreneurial journey, you can lead a truly fulfilling and meaningful life.

RK. Iskandar

As the final pages of this book turn, it's time to reflect on the incredible journey you've embarked upon as a Shopify entrepreneur. From the very beginning, you had a vision, a dream of building a thriving e-commerce empire. You delved into the depths of knowledge, learning the ins and outs of Shopify, mastering the art of marketing, and honing your entrepreneurial skills.

Through the ups and downs, the triumphs and challenges, you persevered with unwavering determination. You embraced the mindset of a successful entrepreneur, conquering self-doubt and pushing through obstacles. You identified your niche, conducted market research, and carefully curated a collection of products that resonated with your target audience.

With your Shopify store as your canvas, you unleashed your creativity, customizing every aspect to create a captivating and user-friendly shopping experience. You optimized your product pages, crafted compelling marketing copy, and strategically designed your checkout process to maximize conversions. Every element of your store was meticulously crafted to entice and engage customers.

Your customers were not just numbers on a screen; they were real individuals with hopes, dreams, and needs. You built a community around your brand, engaging with your customers, and nurturing relationships that extended beyond transactions. Your dedication to exceptional customer service and building trust earned you loyal advocates who spread the word about your business.

You navigated the ever-changing landscape of e-commerce, embracing the latest trends and innovations. You leveraged social media, paid advertising, and email marketing to drive traffic and sales. Your SEO efforts placed you at the top of search engine rankings, and your A/B testing optimized your store's performance. Analytics became your compass, guiding you toward continuous improvement.

As your business flourished, you faced new challenges and opportunities. You expanded your operations, hiring talented individuals who shared your vision and contributed to your growth. You managed cash flow, negotiated with suppliers, and maintained strong relationships with fellow entrepreneurs. Legal and regulatory hurdles were tackled head-on, ensuring compliance and a secure foundation for your business.

Through it all, you never lost sight of yourself—the person behind the entrepreneur. You prioritized self-care, nurturing your physical and mental well-being. You found a balance between work and personal life, cherishing moments with loved ones and cultivating meaningful connections. And amidst the chaos of entrepreneurship, you discovered a profound sense of purpose—a purpose that extended beyond profits and impacted lives.

Now, as you reach this epic ending, you stand as a testament to the possibilities that lie within each aspiring entrepreneur. You have built a successful business, not just in terms of financial gain, but in terms of personal fulfillment and making a difference. Your legacy is not measured solely by the millions of dollars you've made but by the lives you've touched, the communities you've uplifted, and the positive change you've brought to the world.

But this is not the end of your journey; it is only the beginning of a new chapter. Armed with the knowledge, experience, and resilience you've gained, you have the power to continue growing, evolving, and creating an even greater impact.

As you close this book, take a moment to appreciate how far you've come. Embrace the lessons learned, the challenges overcome, and the victories celebrated. Let the experiences of this journey serve as a guiding light as you embark on future endeavors.

You are not just an entrepreneur; you are a visionary, a changemaker, and a force to be reckoned with. The world is yours for the taking, and your Shopify business has laid the foundation for your continued success.

So go forth, inspire others, and create a legacy that will endure for generations to come. The world needs more Shopify entrepreneurs like you—bold, innovative, and driven to make a difference.

Congratulations on completing this epic journey, and may your entrepreneurial spirit continue to thrive as you shape the future with passion, purpose, and an unwavering commitment to excellence

RK. Iskandar

RK. Iskandar